WEBCOMICS 2.0

AN INSIDER'S GUIDE TO WRITING, DRAWING, AND PROMOTING YOUR OWN WEBCOMICS

Steve Horton | Sam Romero

Course Technology PTR
A part of Cengage Learning

COURSE TECHNOLOGY
CENGAGE Learning™

Australia, Brazil, Japan, Korea, Mexico, Singapore, Spain, United Kingdom, United States

COURSE TECHNOLOGY
CENGAGE Learning

Webcomics 2.0: An Insider's Guide to Writing, Drawing, and Promoting Your Own Webcomics
Steve Horton and Sam Romero

Publisher and General Manager, Course Technology PTR: Stacy L. Hiquet

Associate Director of Marketing: Sarah Panella

Manager of Editorial Services: Heather Talbot

Marketing Manager: Jordan Casey

Executive Editor: Kevin Harreld

Project Editor: Dan Foster, Scribe Tribe

Technical Reviewer: Tim Demeter

PTR Editorial Services Coordinator: Erin Johnson

Copy Editor: Gene Redding

Interior Layout Tech: Bill Hartman

Cover Designer: Mike Tanamachi

Indexer: Larry Sweazy

For product information and technology assistance, contact us at
Cengage Learning Customer & Sales Support Center, 1-800-354-9706

For permission to use material from this text or product, submit all requests online at **cengage.com/permissions** Further permissions questions can be emailed to **permissionrequest@cengage.com**

Library of Congress Catalog Card Number: 2007939375

ISBN-10: 1-59863-462-3

ISBN-13: 978-1-59863-462-4

Course Technology
25 Thomson Place
Boston, MA 02210
USA

Cengage Learning is a leading provider of customized learning solutions with office locations around the globe, including Singapore, the United Kingdom, Australia, Mexico, Brazil, and Japan. Locate your local office at: **international.cengage.com/region**

Cengage Learning products are represented in Canada by Nelson Education, Ltd.

For your lifelong learning solutions, visit **courseptr.com**

Visit our corporate website at **cengage.com**

Printed in the United States of America
1 2 3 4 5 6 7 11 10 09 08

To Lori and Andrew, with all my love.

—Steve Horton

I dedicate this book to my mother, Emma Linares, who is the strongest person I know and my greatest source of inspiration, to my family in Peru, and to all of my friends who have been my strength and support. You are my true family and my heart. This is for you.

—Sam Romero

Acknowledgments

Hey, we made it!

This project could not have been accomplished without the following people: Matt Wagner at Fresh Books, Wondrous artist Sam Romero, Kevin Harreld at Course Technology PTR, Dan Foster of Scribe Tribe, technical editor Tim Demeter, webcomics creators T Campbell, David Willis, Howard Tayler, Jennie Breeden, Steve Napierski, Phil and Kaja Foglio, Jeph Jacques, Sarah Ellerton, Chris Crosby, and the Chemistry Set crew (Steven Goldman, Vito Delsante, Dwight MacPherson and Chris Arrant), webcomics business and professional types Joey Manley, Harold Sipe, Steve Wieck, Mike Miller, Nick Popio, Kurt Brunetto, and Jennifer Babcock, the childhood version of myself, who got me into comics in the first place, the webcomics community at large, and, of course, Lori, Andrew, and Zoey.

—Steve Horton

I'd like to give a shout-out to the Couchist and Irfanist art movements of Central Jersey, the avant-garde genius of the Belgian Couchmaster Thomas Hansen of Piscataway, the unusualness of Irfan Ali of New Brunswickstan, and to my dog Leo for keeping me company as I worked on this book.

—Sam Romero

About the Authors

Steve Horton is the author of *Professional Manga: Digital Storytelling with Manga Studio EX* and is the co-creator of the long-running webcomic *Grounded Angel* and the Image comic book series *Strongarm*. He also runs a comics publishing company, Smashout Comics (www.smashout.net), which publishes digital comics through the Wowio e-book service. Steve lives in Noblesville, IN, with his wife, son, and beagle.

Sam Romero is the creator of the popular webcomic *Edge the Devilhunter*, featured at Graphic Smash (www.graphicsmash.com). His stylistic and narrative flair has been best described by webcomics author T Campbell as "tripped-out East-West fusion." Sam dabbled in political cartooning and illustration briefly in college before dedicating himself full-time to writing and drawing action comics on the Internet. Sam currently resides with his family in New Brunswick, NJ.

Contents

Chapter 1
What Are Webcomics?   1

The 2.0 Experience *1*
What This Book Will Teach You *2*
Hey—It's Business *2*
Three Popular Types *2*

Chapter 2
Humor   3

Video Games *4*
Science Fiction *6*
Autobiography *9*
Pop Culture *12*
The Versus Verses *15*
A Webcomic-Shaped Hole *18*

Chapter 3
Adventure   19

The Drifter *20*
    The Drifter: *Characters* *21*
Shoot First, Ask Questions Later *34*

Chapter 4
Manga   35

The Character's the Thing 36
Edge the Devilhunter 37
   Edge. 37
   Princess Tail. 40
   Zelda the Goth. 41
OEL: Original English Language 46

Chapter 5
Other Types of Webcomics   47

Slice of Life 47
Non-Sequitur and Off the Wall 52
Combining Types. 53

Chapter 6
Gathering the Team   55

One Creator, One Destiny. 55
The Creative Team. 57
Finding Talent 58
   A Fair Exchange. 58
   Sign On the Dotted Line 58
   Stay in Communication 59
   It's a Commitment 59
   Searching the Web for Talent 60

Chapter 7
The Webcomics 2.0 Examples   61

The Versus Verses. 61
The Drifter. 61
Edge the Devilhunter 62

Chapter 8
The Writing   93

The Character Bible. *94*
The Comic Script. *96*
Writing Structure. *104*
   Two Approaches *104*
   The Story Arc. *105*
   Three Act Structure *106*
   Rising Action *107*
   Subplots. *108*
   Flashbacks *109*
Transitioning from One Webcomic to Another *110*
All Write Now *110*

Chapter 9
The Art   113

Drawing a Webcomic: Step by Step *114*
   Thumbnails *117*
   Study the Script *117*
   The Panel Borders *118*
   Pencils Out *118*
   Iced Ink *121*
   Scanning It In. *121*
   Finished Art. *123*
   Color *123*
   Lettering *126*
Saving the Art *133*
   The Bleed. *133*
   Infinite Canvas to Finite Book Page. *134*
Miscellaneous Art *134*
   Art Extras *134*
   Character Profiles *135*
Do the Evolution. *135*
Conclusion. *138*

Chapter 10
Getting Published   139

Webcomics Hosting Services *142*
    ComicSpace *143*
    ComicGenesis *144*
    DrunkDuck *144*
    LiveJournal *145*
Webcomics Collectives *146*
    Keenspot *146*
    Blank Label Comics *148*
    Modern Tales *149*
    ACT-I-VATE *149*
    The Chemistry Set *150*
Self-Publishing *154*
    Choosing a Web Host *154*
    Hard Coding *155*
A Final Note on Publishing *156*

Chapter 11
Promotion   157

No-Cost Promotion *158*
    A Community of Potential Fans *158*
    The Power of the Press *163*
Low-Cost Promotion *168*
    Store and Convention Signings *168*
    A Book Tour *169*
    The Expense *170*
    Buying Ad Space on Another Site *170*
A Final Note on Promotion *182*

Chapter 12
Making Money   183

Revenue-Generating Objects *183*
    Advertising *184*
    Google AdSense *184*
    Project Wonderful *185*
    Merchandise *186*
    Books *189*
    Downloadables *193*
Revenue-Generating Locations *206*
    Your Website *206*
    Convention Sales *207*

Chapter 13
The Future of Comics   209

A Large, Untapped Audience *209*
Become Financially Self-Sufficient *210*
The Hardest Thing About Webcomics *210*

Glossary   215

Index   227

1

What Are Webcomics?

What is a webcomic? Simply put, a webcomic is a comic book or comic strip that can be found on the Internet, specifically the World Wide Web. Webcomics are not anti-print comics. That bears repeating: Webcomics and print comics are not exclusionary. In fact, many publishers have found that a Web presence and a print presence are complementary. Fans check out a webcomic and go to a bookstore or comic store to find the print edition. Or fans pick up a comic book or print edition and hit the Web for more comics or background information on their favorite characters.

Webcomics are simply another avenue, and an important one, for comics. The Web is like the ultimate printing press. It's also the ultimate advertising, promotion, and revenue engine for comics, and it cannot be overlooked.

The 2.0 Experience

You may or may not have heard of Web 2.0—that's the nickname for the new do-it-yourself nature of many websites. YouTube lets people upload and share videos. MySpace allows people to show off themselves and get in touch with people. LiveJournal lets people tell the world about their thoughts and feelings.

Webcomics are an extension of that idea, as their very nature as a creative enterprise means they fit into this Web 2.0 model easily. Webcomics put together with Web 2.0 makes Webcomics 2.0, hence the title of this book.

What This Book Will Teach You

What we're going to do here is explain to you how you can write, draw and publish your own webcomic on the Internet. We'll also talk about promotion, merchandising, and making money from your creation: what avenues let you retain full control, what avenues take some of that control in exchange for other benefits, and how you need to protect yourself with contracts.

Hey—It's Business

Though webcomics are ultimately creative, it's important to treat them like a business. Be professional in all levels and stages, as a business should. Ultimately, your creativity and professionalism and the tips in this book will help your webcomic achieve the success and popularity you crave.

Three Popular Types

We're going to start by covering three popular types of webcomics: humor, adventure, and manga. These aren't necessarily the *most* popular types. Rather, they're types that represent familiar ground that a lot of webcomics cover. We're also including three webcomic examples, one of each type. At the end of each example is a web address. You can go to each address and see these webcomics progressing in real time, to help illustrate to you how a webcomic works.

2

Humor

Has anyone ever e-mailed you a link to a webcomic? Odds are, they sent it to you because it was funny and relevant. Many of the best and most popular webcomics on the net, like many newspaper comic strips, are purely humor based or contain strong humor elements. Unlike newspaper strips, though, humor webcomics are not confined to three or four postage stamp–size panels. Humor webcomics are also not subject to the sensibilities of newspaper demographics, which can skew much older than the average webcomics fan, and are not subject to severe restrictions on content imposed by newspapers and print syndicates. Many creators use the canvas of the Web to create comics of all shapes and sizes—sometimes varying that size from day to day!

Humor comes in infinite forms in webcomics, but as far as popularity goes, subject matter has seemed to settle on several distinct forms. That's not to say that you have to fit into one of those niches. In fact, the existence of these popular types might serve as a warning to try something different—or risk drowning in a sea of look-alikes!

Video Games

Video game humor is a frequent topic of webcomics. Why is that? Simply put, gamers use the Internet frequently, and frequent Internet users are often gamers. Also, the same creativity that drives gamers to win also empowers them to write and draw.

There are dozens of video-game webcomics that lampoon the industry, use video games as a backdrop for situation comedy, and even tell funny stories from within a particular video game world.

There is tremendous depth and breadth among the video-game webcomics subgenre. Following are four examples that are about as different as webcomics can be from one another and still have something to do with video games.

The most popular video game webcomic—and one of the most popular webcomics on the entire Internet—is called *Penny Arcade* (www.penny-arcade.com). Drawn by Mike Krahulik and written by Jerry Holkins, otherwise known as Gabe and Tycho, *Penny Arcade* has spawned a yearly convention called the Penny Arcade Expo, a game charity drive for children's hospitals called Child's Play, and a series of reprint books through Dark Horse Comics.

Another popular webcomic, *PvP* by Scott Kurtz (www.pvponline.com), began life as video game humor before morphing into a situation comedy/general pop culture humor strip.

VG Cats, created by Scott Ramsoomair (www.vgcats.com), is a well-drawn video game strip starring anthropomorphic cats that spends its time satirizing specific video game titles.

And then there's Steve Napierski's *Dueling Analogs* (see sidebar), which is almost entirely single-gag strips with wicked satire against video games. But even this one has a recurring cast.

Bottom line is—there are a lot of them, and many are popular, but many aren't. Diving into this world would require you to find a niche that's not already filled. Don't just copy an existing comic. If you can discover a unique angle in video game humor, go for it.

The Webcomics 2.0 Interview: *Dueling Analogs*

Steve Napierski has carved out a niche in the crowded video game humor webcomic world with his acerbic, edgy, and satirical take on all things videogame related: Dueling Analogs (www.duelinganalogs.com). And he's managed to find an audience. Publicly available statistics show Napierski's site averages about 100,000 pageviews per day, and *Dueling Analogs* has an active community.

In July and August 2006, Firaxis Games made a deal with *Dueling Analogs* and only a few other gaming webcomics to run webcomics in support of their new game expansion: *Civilization IV: Beyond the Sword*.

The interviewee is Steve Napierski, creator of Dueling Analogs.

Webcomics 2.0: How did *Dueling Analogs* come to be?

Steve Napierski: I was already working on another webcomic called *The Outer Circle*, which was very story driven, and I wanted to do something else. Something gaming related. Thus, *Dueling Analogs* was born.

WC20: There are a lot of gaming-related webcomics out there—but you've managed to find an audience in spite of that. What's your secret?

SN: Three things…First, the comics are self-encapsulated. That way, whether you start at strip one or strip one hundred, it doesn't matter. Second, it's about video games, their culture, and their community. A lot of other comics start with this but then stray from the formula. With *Dueling Analogs*, it's about gaming and always will be. Lastly, the bright colors. Just look at the huge success of *The Simpsons*.

WC20: Do you have any advice for new webcomics creators interested in the subject of video game humor?

SN: My advice for any person who wants to do a webcomic is simple. The hardest part about doing a webcomic is to actually do a webcomic. After that, everything else is easy. As far as gaming webcomics, the biggest webcomics on the Internet are gaming webcomics. No matter what you do, expect to be compared to them—at least until you find an audience of your own, and then they'll just tell you that you're ripping off *Penny Arcade*.

WC20: How important is it to have regular characters? Is a "gag-a-day" satire enough?

SN: It honestly depends on the project. My main characters are really just the supporting cast. In *Dueling Analogs*, the game and its characters are the real cast. As far as "gag-a-day" satire, that's been one of the contributing factors to *Dueling Analogs'* success. I think a lot of people fear webcomics with long stories. If you miss a strip, you don't know what's going on, and if you start too late, then the archives could be overwhelming.

WC20: What other projects are you working on?

SN: I currently do another comic called *The Outer Circle*. Besides that, I'm just getting ready for conventions. That's like another job altogether.

Science Fiction

There are many sci-fi parody comics on the Web. Usually, these strips tend to focus on ships or crews in space discovering wacky situations, in a kind of riff on *Star Trek* or *Star Wars*. Good examples of humor in a sci-fi vein include Steve Troop's *Melonpool* (www.melonpool.com), Pete Abrams' *Sluggy Freelance* (www.sluggy.com), and Kristofer Straub's *Starslip Crisis* (www.starslipcrisis.com).

Possibly the longest-running of these and one of the most popular is Howard Tayler's *Schlock Mercenary* (see sidebar), about a team of spacefaring mercenaries.

The Webcomics 2.0 Interview: *Schlock Mercenary*

How many other webcomics can claim to run for eight years straight? *Schlock Mercenary* (www.schlockmercenary.com) is one of the only ones, and Howard Tayler's been drawing it the entire time. It's a humor science-fiction strip that rewards devoted readership.

Schlock Mercenary was originally self published by Tayler, who then joined webcomics collective Keenspot for a time. It went independent again and finally landed with another collective, Blank Label Comics.

Tayler has been doing brisk business with print collections of his extensive *Schlock Mercenary* archives. He's one of the many who have proven that webcomics and print comics are synergistic, not exclusionary.

Webcomics 2.0: For new initiates, tell me a little bit about *Schlock Mercenary.*

Howard Tayler: *Schlock Mercenary* is a daily comic strip about a mercenary company in the far future. It's got hard science, hand-wavy science, laugh-out-loud punchlines, and more than its share of bad puns.

I began creating it back in March of 2000, and it has been running every day since June 12 of that year. Lately the site serves up over a quarter-million pages each day and boasts more than 40,000 regular readers.

WC20: How important is it to have regular characters, running gags, and other such elements that keep readers coming back?

HT: Well… I guess since I've never done things any other way, I can't answer based on my experience alone. It's possible that regular characters and running gags will turn away new readers, so there might be a trade-off. I suspect, however, that like any good piece of fiction, *Schlock Mercenary* appeals to readers because it is character driven. It isn't about the technology, or the astronomy, or the politics, or the satire. It is about people the readers can relate to, even if those people have too many arms, or not enough arms, or act like sphincters, or don't have sphincters.

WC20: You released a book collection dating from the strip's relaunch and then decided to publish the earlier strips and renumber the volumes. What prompted this decision?

HT: Ah, the old stuff. How my eyes bleed.

My original plan was for print collections to be widely distributed to bookstores and to sit on shelves. I cringed at the thought of some uninitiated window-shopper picking up a book full of my early artwork. So I decided to find a good starting point with decent artwork and only print books forward from there.

The old stuff would, under this original plan, always remain online, and maybe be put into a collection on CD-ROM.

Well, to make a long story quite short, Sandra and I figured out that we could make a lot more money a lot faster by selling books directly to our readers. We almost went broke launching our little publishing business, but now it pays the bills quite handily, or hand-to-mouthily, at any rate. At that point I saw no reason to not put the old stuff in print. People kept e-mailing me and asking for it, so I went out on a limb and ordered up the most expensive of my print runs to date. Thus far it has paid off—we grossed 25% more on this latest round of pre-orders than we have on any of the others. Our net profits are eerily flat, within 5% of earlier print runs, thanks to the much higher production cost of this latest volume.

I guess if I had to sum up the decision in one sentence, that sentence would go like this: I thought the old stuff would hurt me financially if I put it in print, but I found out I could sell it and make money, so I did.

WC20: Wikipedia seems to have a vendetta against webcomics, including yours specifically, and yet, in 2007, they solicited you for donations. Can you tell me what that whole situation's about, and what Wikipedia can do to make it right?

HT: Wikipedia has no vendettas, though some editors and admins do have agendas. When a Wikinews reporter approached me about the Wikimedia Foundation's donation drive, I took the opportunity to explain my displeasure with these editors and admins and the policies and procedures they exploit. Brian McNeil, the reporter, has no connection with the Foundation or Wikipedia and had no idea that he was stepping on a landmine.

He decided to report on the abuses, and I decided to blog about his report. The *Schlock Mercenary* article has never been at risk during this process, and renown, notability, and personal publicity have never been my objectives. I simply want Wikipedia to be more inclusive. Article deletion is not a tool for making articles better. It's a tool for offending and alienating contributors. "Notability" is not a measuring stick for article inclusion. It's a weapon wielded by elitist editors and admins who one can easily envision coveting a job writing for a *real* encyclopedia.

So I blogged, and Brian reported, and Slash dotted, and I've gotten lots of e-mail from people who said, in essence, "Amen, brother. Wikipedia can't have my money, either." I hope the Wikimedia Foundation sits up and takes notice, because I like to use their encyclopedia for a wide range of things—from particle physics to the niches of modern culture. It would be a shame to see that repository limited by the egos of a few tin-pot dictators.

WC20: What other projects are you working on?

HT: I'm working on a couple of really cool projects with Blank Label Comics right now. Unfortunately, the timing kind of hinges on some legalese and a partnership or two, so I can't say more in this interview.

Schlock fans will be pleased to hear that I'm starting work on the second volume of "the old stuff" this month: *Schlock Mercenary: The Teraport Wars*, which will include all the strips from November 2001 through March 8th, 2003, not to mention the usual raft of bonus material.

The first volume of old stuff, *Schlock Mercenary: The Tub of Happiness*, is still being printed. My advance copies arrive today or tomorrow, and the rest of the copies board a boat and sail from China sometime next week. And then I get to sketch in over 1,200 books. I did the math. These things weigh almost two pounds each. I will quite literally be signing a ton of books.

Autobiography

Autobiographical or semi-autobiographical humor strips are those that take the creator's life and make it more interesting for fiction. By dramatizing and humorizing elements that the creator sees and hears in his daily life, a realness and an unrealness merge to create a greater whole. Think of them as the visual counterpart to a personal blog.

One popular autobiographical webcomic is the appropriately named *Real Life*, by Greg Dean (www.reallifecomics.com).

Another good example of this type is Jennie Breeden's *The Devil's Panties* (see sidebar).

The Webcomics 2.0 Interview: *The Devil's Panties*

One of the most popular female-created and female-focused webcomics, *The Devil's Panties* (www.thedevilspanties.com) is not at all like it sounds. It's a wickedly humorous gag strip about characters that are analogous to creator Jennie Breeden and her friends. Her real life is distilled and warped and given fantasy elements and punchlines, and the comic strip is born.

The Devil's Panties is also innovative in its use of spot color, specifically red for Breeden's character's favorite pair of knee-high flame boots.

The first collected edition of *The Devil's Panties* was released at the end of 2007 from Archaia Studios, and by all accounts is a big hit.

Webcomics 2.0: There are more and more women creating webcomics and more and more women reading them, as opposed to print comics, which are still largely male centered. What are your thoughts on this?

Jennie Breeden: I majored in Sequential Art at Savannah College of Art and Design, so I started off on the print side of comics. I worked at a comic shop in Atlanta and, yes, the customers were mostly adult male, but more and more women are getting into comics. This is largely due to manga. There are a lot of Japanese comics that are written specifically for women—stories about school and friendship with nothing about super powers or world domination. There are a lot of comics by Vertigo that are universal and pull a lot of non-comic fans into the stores. *Fables* and *Runaways* are the top pick for anyone, boy or girl, who wouldn't normally be into comic books.

There were not as many women in comics because we didn't have very much to identify with in the industry. Most of the publishers just threw in a female to a spandex team and thought that would be enough. Now there are more and more women reading comics and, therefore, drawing comics. We're creating comics that we're interested in. I'm finding that people all over the world, male or female, are interested in a lot of the same things that I am. I do cartoons about things that I think are weird or unique, and I get e-mails from all over the world from people who like the same thing. It's all a question of seeing ourselves in a story. Women can't really identify with Superman (though I'm a Batman kinda girl) but we can get into *Girls with Slingshots* or *Wapsi Square*.

WC20: *The Devil's Panties* is somewhat autobiographical. How difficult is it to translate real-life situations into something that's funny and interesting for the comic?

JB: I never really know what's going to make a good comic strip until I sit down to draw it. Some stories don't make very good comics, and some comic strips don't make for very good stories. Comics are a balance of words and pictures. A good comic has its words and pictures work off one another. The pictures have to react well with the text. I've had experiences that are funny and make great stories, but I could never fit them into the frames of a comic.

There are some comics that were based on something that wasn't very funny at the time, but when I put it into the boxes of a comic strip, something in it just clicked. I take some liberties with the autobiographical part. Life isn't as exaggerated as it is in my comic strip, but sometimes, to get the idea across, I embellish a little. In real life I'm nowhere near as energetic or spastic as I am in the comic strip. Most of the time the punchline in my comics is what I wish I had said or done at the time. It's a lot of fun to have your own reality to play with.

WC20: One of your only colors in the strip is red. How do you decide what gets to be red?

JB: I tried coloring the strip, but I'm not too good at that. My sister told me to stop putting all the colors in and just do one or two. I like what *Herobear* does with his one red cape, so I use red for my flame boots. Each regular character has their own one color. My boyfriend has a T-shirt with a light blue smiley face. The shoulder devil has red wings, angel has a yellow halo, pretty princess has pink. It's one of the many liberties of publishing online. No extra cost for color.

WC20: Your statements on how to make it as a webcartoonist in your FAQ have been widely circulated. Has this actually had an effect on any aspiring comics creators?

JB: Widely circulated? Really? Cool. I don't look around much online; I spend most of my time drawing the comic strip. I got a lot of support from other webcomic artists when I was starting out, so I try to pass that forward. There have been a few who said that they started doing a webcomic because of encouragement that I gave them. But doing a webcomic is something that the individual has to decide on. It's one of the hardest things out there. It takes a lot of work, and the only reward, starting out, is simply people reading it. You can get all the encouragement you want from outside sources, but in the end, it's just a question of your own drive.

WC20: What other projects are you working on?

JB: There's *The Devil's Panties* graphic novel that is coming out through Archaia Press in April. I draw five cartoons a day, and only one of those strips goes up online. The rest go into the comic book. There's also the LARPing comic that I do on www.geebasonparade.com and the vampire comic that's for an online vampire magazine at www.vampirerave.com/bw. There's also illustrations that I do for short stories at fromtheasylum.com, and I'm commissioned to illustrate the cartoons for www.customerssuck.com/strip.

Pop Culture

Finally, there's pop culture humor, which is where our webcomic example fits. Just like it sounds, pop culture humor webcomics make fun of whatever's popular.

One important pop-culture humor webcomic has made enormous gains in popularity and readership in a very short time. It's called *xkcd*, and it's created by X. Through the use of science, romance, and math-based humor, as well as iconic stick figures, X has reached an untapped audience in the hundreds of thousands.

Another pop-culture strip, *Shortpacked!,* by David Willis (see sidebar), lampoons toy retail, including those who work there, those who shop there, and the toys themselves. It also takes time for one-off gag comics about some element of pop culture, usually Batman, GI Joe, or Transformers.

The Webcomics 2.0 Interview: *Shortpacked!*

David Willis is one of the pioneers of webcomics. He's one of those guys who did a comic strip in high school and college and then just kept drawing, and drawing, and drawing. *Roomies!*, a humor strip about college life, ran from 1997 to 1999—at one point, it ran in the *Indiana Daily Student* and on the Web simultaneously, one of the first to appear both in print and online at the same time. *It's Walky!*, a science-fiction sequel (with a mixture of humor and drama), succeeded it, running from 1999 to 2004.

Shortpacked! (www.shortpacked.com) is the current incarnation. Though ostensibly an off-the-wall humor webcomic about toy retail and pop culture, *Shortpacked!* occasionally has dramatic elements to offset the humor.

Also, two of the main characters from *It's Walky!* continue in an ongoing subscription webcomic called *Joyce & Walky* (www.itswalky.com).

All of Willis' webcomics take place in the same universe, which fans have dubbed the Walkyverse. This universe has been around for over a decade and is still going strong. Willis keeps gaining in popularity. Though once a part of Keenspot, Willis and several others now form the collective Blank Label Comics. This collective is often the top money earner on advertising site Project Wonderful, and Willis is a major contributor to that success. Here's what he has to say about it all.

Webcomics 2.0: You've been in the webcomics biz for over 10 years. About how long did it take before you felt webcomics were able to support you all on its own?

David Willis: My first brush with self-employment was a happy accident. Several years ago, I was working retail at a Warner Bros Studio Store, and when AOL merged with Time Warner, that store was one of the first things to go. Basically, I survived for a few months off Ramen noodles, until I realized I could sell my art and make money. At the time, though, I didn't have as many dedicated readers, as I needed to support myself long-term, so when my car blew a brake pad a few years later, I had to get a job at Toys "R" Us to help pay the bills. Armed with this knowledge, however, I confidently left TRU a few years later to make it work for real.

It certainly couldn't happen without building up that readership first. I don't think you can just start making money right out of the gate. If you have fewer than 10,000 readers, I say forget it, unless you [have] a handful of really generous sugar-daddies. Even so, it's not always the number of readers you have. You could have 25,000 readers who only like you a little. The percentage of those who like your strip better than anything else they read will determine how successful you'll be supporting yourself. And finally, you have to have the determination to make it possible. For example, I'm determined to stay home and watch cartoons.

WC20: *Shortpacked!* seems to veer wildly between humor, non-sequitur, and even drama. Is there any particular reason you switch gears when you do?

DW: I like to keep myself interested. If I'm going to draw a comic strip every other day for the foreseeable future, it has to engage all areas of my creative instincts. Nothing's more frustrating to me than an idea I can't implement. Like our intrepid Native American friends, I like to use all parts of the buffalo.

That perspective is, by my own admission, an immature one. There has to be some focus, so I temper my madness with a few unspoken rules about *Shortpacked!*'s universe that I never violate. Boundaries are important.

WC20: Joyce and Walky is one of the few webcomics to make the subscription model work. How did you pull it off?

DW: It was only possible because I drew *Roomies!/ It's Walky!* for seven years, completed it, and then shelved it. Apparently, that then creates consumer demand. It's not a business model I think I can recommend. "Okay, first draw a seven-year story for free." It's just not practical in the short term, which is what people want. If you plan to market a new strip with the subscription-only model, you'd better either be a household name or be happy with making grocery money.

WC20: Your original strip, *Roomies!*, *It's Walky!*, *Shortpacked!*, and *Joyce and Walky* all reside in the same universe and even share characters. Do you see all your projects following from this, or will you ever create something totally unrelated?.

DW: It's possible that some day in the future I'll have written myself into a corner, with nowhere else in the "Walkyverse" to pin down and explore. It was important when ending *It's Walky!*, a strip with a mythology that was so pervasive in its own universe, to start anew someplace in the middle of nowhere. Someplace mundane. It had to be new territory. I can see myself telling more mundane stories in the *It's Walky!* universe, potentially forever.

If I did another epic, though, it would have to be a new universe.

WC20: What other projects are you working on?

DW: For the moment, *Shortpacked!* satisfies all areas of my brain. I've flirted with rebooting *Roomies!/It's Walky!* and doing another series with them in college, but that would take time away from *Shortpacked!*, and I'd have to choose. As of now, *Shortpacked!* wins.

The Versus Verses

And now we come to our webcomics example. Created by webcomics writer T Campbell and used with permission, and drawn by *Webcomics 2.0* artist Sam Romero, *The Versus Verses* takes two pop culture characters or elements that happen to sound alike and puts them in a rhyming duel. Sounds strange? It is, but oddly, it works. *The Versus Verses* satirizes everything from *Harry Potter* and *Welcome Back Kotter* to *Calvin & Hobbes* and *Alvin and the Chipmunks* (see the rhyme?).

Romero started with pencil art (Figure 2.1), inked it (Figure 2.2), and finally created a final color drawing, coloring in a Sunday newspaper comic style (Figure 2.3).

The full *The Versus Verses* comics can be found at the center of this book. You'll notice that *Versus Verses* doesn't limit itself to a single format, often rearranging its panels in multiple directions. This is an example of "infinite canvas," or using the medium of the Web to create webcomics of any direction and size. Here's a look at the preliminary versions, so you can see how Romero got to the finished drawing.

Figure 2.1 Calvin vs. Alvin begins with a pencil drawing.

Figure 2.2 The strip is then inked with a pen or brush. The figures take on form and definition.

Figure 2.3 Finally, the strip is colored in Adobe Photoshop and lettered in Adobe Illustrator.

A Webcomic-Shaped Hole

Humor webcomics, in large part, serve an audience different than that served by newspaper strips. Humor webcomics fans are younger and more interested in Internet culture. These fans like online gaming, blogging, MySpace, and satire. They like their entertainment to bite back at them. Webcomics creators have responded to that need and have created humor strips that would not belong anywhere else but on the Web. You can, too.

3

Adventure

One of many great things about webcomics is that space is not a consideration. The size of the screen is all that matters. Though some have experimented with infinite-space comics that scroll in multiple directions (see Chapter 2), adventure webcomics creators often stick to a single page, either horizontal or vertical in format, so that an adventure comic looks like the classic Sunday adventure serials. You know the ones I'm talking about: *Flash Gordon. Steve Canyon. Terry and the Pirates. The Spirit.* Or, the adventure comic looks like a comic book page. Again, the nature of the Web means this is far from a requirement.

Adventure comics have strong protagonists, rollicking adventure, death, destruction, explosions, and cool chase scenes. Adventure webcomics are clearly critical favorites and have won awards. Such comics can find an audience, especially if they tread ground not explored before and do it with good, clear storytelling, technically sound art, and unobtrusive coloring.

Adventure comics can take place in any time period and setting, as long as there are adventures to be had. Western, classic or modern science fiction, superhero, kung fu, battling magicians, horror, sword and sorcery—the possibilities are limitless.

Some adventure webcomics stick to a traditional three- or four-panel black-and-white comic strip for weekdays and then go all out in lavish color on Sundays, attempting to stick as closely as possible to the traditional format. Others prefer to publish one to three times a week and go for that horizontal Sunday-esque look each and every time. Others go for a comic book page style. Some don't do any of these. It all depends on how hard you and your team feel like working. Keep in mind that regular updates are one of the ways to build an audience.

The Drifter

Here's an example of an adventure serial. It's called *The Drifter*, and it takes the form of the 1970s and 1980s television detective dramas. These stories always featured a strong loner private detective whose weakness was the inability to stay in one place for long. This tall, dark, and handsome stranger (two out of three ain't bad, in some cases) would therefore travel to a new locale every episode and solve a crime, making things right before he has to move on. Sometimes he'd be chased by the authorities, who could never quite catch up with him. Sometimes the hero would ultimately be searching for something or someone and need to make the world better in the meantime.

Examples of this genre on TV included *The Fugitive*, *The Incredible Hulk*, *Magnum P.I.*, *The Rockford Files*, *MacGyver*, and *Spenser: For Hire*. Note that some of these examples don't include the all-important drifting aspect, but they include enough of the important *ronin*, or masterless samurai, element to draw inspiration from.

The Drifter is a new take on the *ronin*, but in the modern day. This bounty hunter/detective travels from city to city, town to town, cleaning up messes and fixing lives—for a price. The man with the mysterious past never stays long, but he always leaves an impression. Most are grateful, but some don't appreciate his meddling, and that's why he always has to leave. Also, someone is chasing him.

The Drifter: Characters

Here are the two main characters in *The Drifter* and their antagonist.

The Drifter is Pete Kincaid. He goes by Kincaid, always. Only a few souls are trusted (or mistrusted) with his first name, including his lovely assistant and the man chasing him. The Drifter is a smiling, sardonic, ladies' man. His charisma, his wits, his two fists, and his Colt 1911 are what get him through the day—that and successfully solving a crime. He's a detective with no agency, a traveler with no destination. He's The Drifter. As shown in Figure 3.1, he originally had an older, weathered appearance. This didn't turn out to fit the character's personality, so we drew a younger but still firmly 1980s character instead. Figure 3.2 through 3.4 show the progression between the pencil, inked, and color art for the final Kincaid.

Figure 3.1

The original look for The Drifter was deemed too *Matlock.*

Figure 3.2
This is more like it. Sam Romero changed his face and created the perfect Kincaid.

Figure 3.3
The Kincaid draw-
ing is inked and
begins to take form.

Figure 3.4
Finally, Kincaid is
brought to life in
TV color.

The Assistant is Jennifer Lancaster. She considers herself a full partner in the Kincaid detective agency, but she has a difficult time convincing Kincaid that she's anything more than his able assistant. She's solved several cases on her own or discovered the crucial piece of evidence that Kincaid overlooked. Lancaster and Kincaid's relationship is complicated. The only thing Lancaster will admit is that they're business associates, nothing more. And yet, she's willing to travel with him from place to place. Does she have an ulterior motive—or more than one? Figures 3.5 through 3.7 show Lancaster as the art moves toward full color.

Figure 3.5 Lancaster was exactly right from this first drawing.

Figure 3.6 Characters from *T.J. Hooker* and even *Who's the Boss?* were used as inspiration for Lancaster.

Figure 3.7
It was Sam Romero's idea to make her a brunette.

The G-Man's real name is unknown. He appears only in the shadows, with his huge reflective glasses the only thing visible. He's often present in the background, waiting for the right moment to catch Kincaid. The G-Man once worked for a client of Kincaid's. The job went wrong, the G-Man wants Kincaid dead, and the manhunt consumes his life.

The G-Man starts out in Figure 3.8 as a series of sketches to refine his look. In Figure 3.9, a full-body pencil shot is decided on. It's inked in Figure 3.10 and colored in Figure 3.11. In Figures 3.12 through 3.14, a profile shot of the same G-Man is depicted. We can see what he looks like close up, even if our main characters haven't a clue.

Figure 3.8
Sam Romero drew a number of sketches before deciding on The G-Man's look.

Figure 3.9
Having settled on his appearance, Romero pencils a full-body shot.

Figure 3.10
The G-Man is more heavily inked and shadowed compared to the other characters.

Figure 3.11
The G-Man doesn't need much color to define him.

Figure 3.12
Romero says that
the G-Man is his
favorite character to
draw. Here's a head
shot.

Figure 3.13
Again, the G-Man
is heavily inked.

Figure 3.14
A bit of color
rounds things out.

An original short story, "The Drifter: Pilot" can be found in the center of this book. Though this is likely the only place you'll be able to read the pilot of *The Drifter*, continuing adventures of *The Drifter* and his detective agency are available online at www.comicspace.com

Shoot First, Ask Questions Later

Adventure webcomics are critical favorites because they're often the home of involving character arcs and compelling, grounded characters. It's not about the awards, though. It's about satisfying a need in your soul for action. This action is given form and purpose in the adventure webcomic.

4

Manga

One of the most dominant types of webcomics on the Net is manga. *Manga* is the Japanese word for comics, and manga therefore are Japanese comics. This definition has also been extended to mean comics created by non-Japanese in a similar style. Extraordinarily popular among readers of all ages, manga has exerted an enormous influence on young artists. Some manga-esque webcomics utilize only the art style and are otherwise Western in story and content, while some dive straight into Japanese culture and attempt to be Japanese comics in every possible sense.

Webmanga, like print manga, are notable for their iconic but extraordinarily expressive characters, sudden shifts in dramatic tone, use of speed lines, *chibi* (very small versions of characters, expressing extreme emotion), and big sound effects. Since print manga can often stretch across multiple 180-page *tankobon*, or small, digest-size graphic novels, webmanga are also known for their long, drawn-out storylines.

Webmanga are usually presented in vertical comic-page form rather than horizontal comic strips. The dimensions of a webmanga page are proportional to a manga art board, which is 8.3 by 11.7 inches, differing from the American "one and a half up" comic book page dimensions of 11 by 17 inches (so called because it is 1.5 times larger than a printed page). These dimensions make it easy to convert a webmanga into a print collection later.

However, since this is the Web we're talking about, feel free not to limit yourself to the traditional manga page size. Use any size and shape you want, from single panels with large lettering suitable for mobile phones, to infinite canvas manga that stretch in any direction.

The most popular manga-influenced webcomic and one of the most popular webcomics on the face of the planet is called *Megatokyo* (created by Fred Gallagher and Rodney Caston; found at www.megatokyo.com). Though starting out as a humor strip, this particular webcomic is now a romance-infused drama with an enormous female audience. Out of all the types of webcomics, manga is more likely to appeal to women. One of the most common web-manga, *Yaoi*, deals with young men in love with each other. Strangely enough, this subject is extraordinarily popular with girls.

That's not to say that manga isn't for guys, too. In fact, some of the best action sequences, guns, technology, robots, and cool characters can be found in online manga.

The Character's the Thing

One thing that many webmanga have in common is their focus on characterization and personality, rather than plot. The occurrences in a given episode or page are secondary to how the protagonists and antagonists react to them. This means that strong characters with good backgrounds are essential. Fans of popular webmanga tend to latch on to their favorite characters like glue and obsess over them. Obsessive fans can be a double-edged sword, but, overall, they're the best kinds of fans to have because they will stick with you and bring their friends.

Edge the Devilhunter

This example of a webmanga is called *Edge the Devilhunter*, and it's about the bad guys. *Edge the Devilhunter* stars an ensemble cast of humans, angels, and demons who struggle for power in a dystopian rendition of New York City. Much of the action focuses on Jack juggling his various alter egos, their respective responsibilities, and the sometimes disastrous results therein. Shonen manga starring very young protagonists and focusing on action, adventure, fighting, and subtle touches of romance are extremely common in Japan, and this comic adopts many elements of the manga tradition and injects a uniquely American flavor into the mix.

Edge the Devilhunter is *Transmetropolitan* meets *Blue Monday* meets *Das Kapital*. A chaotic young thug finds himself resurrected, with no recollection of previous events in his life, and soon after becomes conscripted by divine forces to make war against the earthbound legions of hell.

Following are the three main characters in *Edge the Devilhunter*.

Edge

Edge, a.k.a. "Jack," a chaotic young thug from Flushing in the Queens borough of New York City, is a member of a rare type of highly-powered, nigh-invulnerable human sub-race commonly referred to as "nexthumans." Despite his freakish genetic talents, he is often a victim of very bad luck and has to rely on his wits rather than his superpowers to weasel out of many bizarre and dicey imbroglios. He is an amnesiac, conscripted by divine entities and sent to battle with the unseen, earthbound agents of hell. In addition to the woes of his enslavement and memory loss, he also reluctantly adopts a strange little girl named Elvy, whose mere thoughts can warp the fabric of reality. His front job is that of personal bodyguard for the very unpleasant tech-crime "queenpin" Princess Tail, to whom he owes a nightmarishly steep debt, having blown up her subterranean palace during their first and last date.

In Figure 4.1, artist Sam Romero began with pencil art of Edge in his civilian and Edge personas. In Figure 4.2, Romero inks and colors the finished drawing.

Figure 4.1
Edge the Devilhunter, in both his civilian and devilhunter guises.

Figure 4.2
The inked and colored finished art.

Princess Tail

Princess Tail, a.k.a. Jasmine Cody, is a ridiculously young player in New York's criminal underworld. She is a "gearhead," a person into the culture of highly illicit cybernetic body modification, and heads a small but fierce gang founded by her late mother, called the Southside Denizens. Her innocent, girly façade masks a fiery temper and idiosyncratic background. She is of Irish and Black descent, but due to a statistical rarity, inherited none of her mother's African features, all of them going to her twin brother, Dawgboy. She is very fond of "40-Bounce" malt liquor and can chug bottles empty in seconds, though her constitution is questionable. Princess Tail meets Jack while seeking revenge against him for frightening children in her gang. She crushes on him instantly and dates him soon after, only to have her home blown up by Jack in a pyrrhic but successful move fending off a formidable assassin.

Princess Tail starts with a pencil sketch (Figure 4.3), and then the bright, gaudy colors and blue tail define her look (Figure 4.4).

Zelda the Goth

Zelda the Goth, a.k.a. Zelda Ricci, is Princess Tail's second-in-command and is primarily responsible for the gang's daily operations. Contrary to everyone's perceptions about the gang's hierarchy, she is actually the one who gets things done and makes all the major decisions. Against Princess Tail's wishes, Zelda uses the gang's destroyed property as a pretense to coerce Jack into becoming Tail's personal bodyguard, seeing his nexthuman powers as an invaluable asset to the gang's roster. Her disposition is that of a misanthropic Goth, and she has an unusually high dislike of men in general, and Jack especially. However, she shares a strong sisterly bond with Princess Tail, having been picked off the street and raised by Tail's mother, the legendary Queen Tail. Zelda makes it top priority to shield Tail from the nastier elements of the underworld and cocoons her in the extreme when the blood starts flying.

Zelda the Goth's pencil drawing is up first (Figure 4.5), and much black is added to the drawing in the color stage (Figure 4.6). There are still hints of other color, such as brown highlights in Zelda's hair and yellow buttons.

An original short story, "Edge the Devilhunter," can be found at the center of this book. This is a completely remastered and redrawn version of the story that originally appeared on webcomics collective Graphic Smash. In this story, our hero is just finishing his demon-slaying duties for the night, and soon after switches back to his civilian persona as bodyguard for an extremely unpleasant black market employer. Read the complete *Edge* story at www.graphicsmash.com!

Figure 4.3
Princess Tail is the leader of the Southside Denizens gang.

Figure 4.4
The inked and colored Princess Tail.

Figure 4.5
Zelda the Goth, the
true force behind
the Southside
Denizens.

Figure 4.6
Mostly black is used in the final color drawing, for obvious reasons.

OEL: Original English Language

If you read tankobon obsessively; attend manga conventions (whether into cosplay or not); watch manga on TV, DVD, and the local anime club, and are bursting with creativity, then a webmanga is your natural outlet. Originality is key, here. Though it's OK to learn to draw using your favorite characters, create something totally your own for the Web. After all, self-ownership is one of the cornerstones of webcomics.

5

Other Types of
Webcomics

Not all webcomics fit into the humor, adventure, and manga categories. There
are two types of webcomics, in fact, that are gaining ground among fans—one
because it offers the same dramatic soap-opera elements that keep people glued
to a good TV drama, and the other because it's totally off the wall, sometimes
funny, sometimes interesting, but always bizarre.

Slice of Life

One major type of webcomic is one that gets its roots in such printed classics
as *Maus* and *American Splendor*. It's more like real life. A soap-opera strip, in
other words. Also known as *slice of life*, these real-life fables are sometimes autobiographical and include characters and situations that might be found in a
typical episode of *Friends* or *Grey's Anatomy*. Or, these dramatic creations mir-
ror explorations of humanity found in the literary works of Nick Hornby or
Michael Chabon, to name two.

A few slice-of-life webcomics, such as *Questionable Content* and *Penny and
Aggie* (see sidebars), are staggeringly popular, as fans follow characters through
their lives for years. Often, if a character dies in the course of the story, it can
be devastating to the fans.

Webcomics 2.0 Interview: *Questionable Content*

A true success story in the world of slice-of-life webcomics, Jeph Jacques' *Questionable Content* (www.questionablecontent.net) has built an enormous audience over its five-year life. *QC* averages somewhere north of 500,000 pageviews per day, and it's all thanks to Jacques' efforts and the characters he's brought to life: introvert and main character, Marten; girl with issues and roommate, Faye; outgoing nice girl, Dora. Plus, don't forget the cute talking computers named Pintsize and Winslow. *QC* is one of the giants, and it's not hard to see why.

The interviewee is Jeph Jacques, creator of *Questionable Content*.

Webcomics 2.0: *Questionable Content* successfully combines slice-of-life and humor. Are there any tips you can offer on how to be funny while still moving the plotlines forward?

Jeph Jacques: I think it's really important to have something in each strip that would be funny to someone who had never read the comic before, didn't know the backstory, didn't know the characters, and so on. That's the hook that will hopefully keep new readers coming back and get them interested in what's actually going on in the strip.

As far as moving plotlines along, I think it's important to take your time and let things develop naturally. It's easy to get impatient and rush things, but small changes over time make for a more satisfying payoff than constant upheaval.

WC20: How important is it for you to have a speculative element in the strip, in the form of Pintsize and Winslow? Does it balance out the realism?

JJ: The robots and other fantastic elements in the strip are kind of like a pressure valve for my brain—I know that if I'm bogged down in an arc or tired of a specific setting, I can ask, "Hey, what are they doing right now?" and it will usually be funny and fun for me to do. They're also a lot easier to draw than all the humans! It gives me a little more freedom to be silly and play up my interests in science fiction and futurism and stuff. Plus, they're cute, and people like cute things.

WC20: How much do you plan in advance and how much is just spur of the moment, while you're drawing the strip?

JJ: I have an overall storyline very vaguely plotted out in my head—ideas about where the story is headed in the long term, how different characters and relationships might evolve, that sort of thing. The day-to-day comics are usually written the night I draw them—if I'm working on a particular arc, I might already know what I'm going to draw subject-wise, but making it "funny" is always a seat-of-the-pants kind of thing. Scripts are getting constantly revised as I draw them, and usually the last panel will go through three or four iterations by the time I get to the lettering and publishing stage.

Basically I know where I want the story to go, and I do what I can to give it nudges in that general direction. But it's never set in stone. I couldn't have predicted the stuff that would've happened around #500 even two months before it happened.

WC20: How long did it take for *QC* to become what you would consider popular? Are there any steps you deliberately took to get it there?

JJ: Well, it became my full time job in September of 2004, and I was getting about 30,000 readers per day at that point if I remember correctly, so I suppose that is as good a "popularity" point as any.

As far as specific stuff I did goes, I became an active member of a bunch of other comics forums—never posting to promote *my* comic, just talking about their stuff, engaging the community and creators. Eventually some of those authors noticed my comic and liked it, so they linked it on their sites, which got me a big traffic boost, which led to more word-of-mouth publicity, which is what gradually got me to the point I'm at today.

WC20: What other projects are you working on?

JJ: I've got my on-again-off-again project Indietits (www.indietits.com), and I play guitar and record music in my spare time. Other than *QC*, that's about it!

Webcomics 2.0 Interview: *Penny and Aggie*

T Campbell and Gisele Lagace's *Penny and Aggie* (www.pennyandaggie.com), a combination humor and slice-of-life web-comic done in sort of a hybrid manga and Western-influenced style, has been going for about four years now. Originally on webcomics invitation-only collective Keenspot, writer Campbell and artist Lagace struck out on their own in January 2007, taking their fans with them. *Penny and Aggie* is the story of popular girl Penny and introverted avant-garde girl Aggie. The webcomic averages about 72,000 pageviews per day, and the comic's forum is extraordinarily popular.

The interviewee is T Campbell, writer of Penny and Aggie.

Webcomics 2.0: How did *Penny and Aggie* get started?

T Campbell: Oddly, Gis and I started working together when I sent her a message about her writing on Cool Cat Studio that amounted to "You're doing it all wrong." Gis was like, "Oh, yeah? Let's see if you can do better."

After dealing with a handful of my scripts, she quit cartooning for two years. Then she suddenly burst into my inbox in 2004, babbling about how she had split her teenage self into two distinct personalities and asking whether I could turn this exercise in mad science into a working comic strip aimed at newspapers.

Three years later, here we are, doing stories about stabbings and rampant lesbianism. King Features Syndicate will be calling any day now.

WC20: *Penny and Aggie* is not the first webcomic you've written, but it's by far the most popular. To what do you attribute its success?

TC: We're filling a need, I think. Our work is wholesome, thoughtful, and honest, which is a rare combination. We're not kewl or skate or whatever the word for "cool" is this week, but we are aware that it's the twenty-first century. Once Gisele gave me the basic specs, I've been trying to use the strip to understand what it's like to be a teenage girl in this day and age, and a lot of people seem to respond to that.

It's more consistent than my other major project, *Fans*, which was hyperthyroidic experimentation. New readers can tell what they're getting into.

Also, Gisele can draw, like, really well.

WC20: How do you and artist Gisele Lagace work together? Do you write in comic script format or discuss plots over e-mail? How does this differ from, say, a print comic book creative team?

TC: The biggest difference is that I'm my own editor, which is good and bad. The writer me thinks I'm a great boss, and the editor me is worried I'm a pushover, except when the editor me is a happy tyrant and the writer me wishes she was a professional surfer instead.

Gisele and I talk basic plots, but we have a lot of faith in each other's ability to do our jobs, and the writing is my job. I do scripts in Microsoft Word, and Gisele draws 'em. I try not to ask for changes too often, because the first sentence in this paragraph is still true.

WC20: What would you say is one of the more challenging aspects of writing webcomics?

TC: Not having whole generations' worth of examples to fall back on. You never know what will work until you try it. This is also one of the more liberating aspects.

WC20: What other projects are you working on?

TC: This is a retro period right now: I'm doing a finale for Cool Cat Studio and a sequel to *Fans*. By the time you publish, Gisele and I will have *Webcomics.com* up, and I'll be doing something so utterly crazy that once I came up with it, there was no way I could avoid it.

Non-Sequitur and Off the Wall

Another popular type of webcomic is the non-sequitur, or off-the-wall strip. These strips sometimes have the exact same art every day (as in Ryan North's Dinosaur Comics at www.dinosaurcomics.com) or have art that is extremely minimalist (Nicholas Gurewitch's Perry Bible Fellowship at www.pbf-comics.com). The point of these comics is not always to be funny, though readers laugh anyway. The point is to be weird and to do it in a way that entertains. Sometimes a non-sequitur comic will produce a quote or saying that will come to life and spread throughout the Internet. This saying can become popular enough to land on a T-shirt or be quoted in many blogs and forum posts.

Off the wall webcomics get by on the strength of their writing, especially dialogue. Since Dinosaur Comics always has the same dinosaurs, it's the bizarre, unreal conversations between the characters that make it fun. A good TV analogy is the old Cartoon Network show *Space Ghost Coast to Coast*. It wasn't always funny, but it was always weird and always entertained.

Perry Bible Fellowship has to be seen to be believed. It satirizes pop culture and kills the characters a lot. One indicator of its popularity is the print edition from Dark Horse Comics, the first volume of which has gone through several printings.

Combining Types

Often, the best webcomics aren't easily pigeonholed into one genre. Successful combination of types can broaden a webcomics' audience and expose it to more readers than one that slavishly sticks to one type. For example, *Shortpacked!* is ostensibly a humor comic about weird employees of a toy store. Once in awhile, creator David Willis puts in an unrelated satire comic, poking fun at an element of pop culture (often Batman, GI Joe, or Transformers) that deserves skewering. And sometimes *Shortpacked!* delves into drama, though it is always self-referential when this happens (characters beating each other up for having too many flashbacks, and so on).

Even the best TV dramas have comedic elements. The best sitcoms sometimes had audience-quieting drama. The webcomic *Megatokyo* (created by Fred Gallagher and Rodney Caston, found at www.megatokyo.com) began as a humor strip and morphed into a drama through the course of its life. If in the course of creating your webcomic you feel the actions and situations yanking the comic from one type into another, just go with it. You just might find a whole new audience waiting for you.

6

Gathering the Team

The first thing to do when gathering your creative team is to assess your skills as a writer and an artist. Show your work to people who aren't in your immediate family or circle of friends. If you find you don't have what it takes, play to your strengths and bring in people who can help you fill those gaps. Though some of the best webcomics are one-person shows, others are teams of two or more. This chapter discusses some of the advantages and disadvantages of both.

One Creator, One Destiny

A sole creator writes the story, draws and letters the comic, manages the comic on the site, and deals with all publicity, marketing, merchandising, and so on, all by himself. This is entirely possible—many have done it—but it can be difficult. The good news is, by the time your webcomic hits it big, you'll ideally have enough clout (or money) to bring on assistants, especially to handle the business side of things. That's down the road, though.

As a single creator, you also reap all the profits from your comic and don't have to share with anyone. Sole webcomics creators have a much smoother road toward supporting themselves because they make more money per person. There's no chance of a partner getting angry and walking away or, worse yet, fighting you for control of the comic. You don't have to depend on anyone but yourself to be successful.

Many single creators don't really write out a script beforehand. They might do a plot or outline and then just start drawing and see where their art takes them. This can mean two things: The storylines are fresh, dynamic, and offbeat, or the storylines are plotless and meandering. Creators might see something in pop culture—or even at the grocery store—and jot down a mental or physical note for later use in the comic, much like a blogger. If it's just you, you don't have to convince anyone else that your idea is worthy. You just do it.

The downside to this is that if your storyline takes a wrong turn, you've got nobody to tell you that what you're doing is going to paint you into a corner or wreck the story. This is why allowing feedback from fans is essential. Though it's never wise to give the fans what they think they want, a surge of negativity or a drop in readership is a good signal that you're heading in the wrong direction.

One solution to this is seeking feedback before publishing each installment of your webcomic. Peers who do their own webcomics can be good judges of what works. Don't discount the opinions of friends and family. Your significant other can also be an excellent choice for keeping your webcomic on the right path.

Most sole creators, like many freelancers, have a job, spouse, trust fund, or other secondary income to keep them afloat while they realize their dream. It's not a good idea to quit your day job to do webcomics. Quitting the job is something to do later, when your comic becomes successful! If you're one of the lucky ones who don't have to work full-time to support your family, you've got a leg up on everyone else simply because you have more time to devote to your dream. You're ahead of the game. However, if you do have a full-time gig and only have nights and weekends to devote to your comic at first, that's OK, too—one of your goals with this book is to maximize the time and energy you do have.

The Creative Team

Working as part of a team on the webcomic is the other option. This method parallels print comic books, in which there is usually one writer, one penciller, one inker, one colorist, and one letterer. Teams on webcomics are generally smaller—two or three at the most. One person does all the writing, plotting, dialogue, and concepts, another does all the art, and then, if there's a third partner, he does the coloring or letters, whichever step the writer or artist can't do him or herself.

The larger webcomics will also have someone to handle business matters and public relations—a manager, in other words. Robert Khoo of Penny Arcade is one prominent example. Khoo's work on the business side frees up creators Mike Krahulik and Jerry Holkins to concentrate on the creative side.

For some of the smaller comics, a spouse or significant other will sometimes help with the merchandising side, such as packing and shipping—a time-consuming process that can take a lot of time away from writing and drawing.

Again, play to your strengths. Don't attempt to draw your comic if you discover that you have little or no skill in art. Fans notice deficiencies, and your popularity will be nonexistent. On the flipside, if you're an extraordinary artist but can't come up with any good ideas, hook up with a writer.

If you're a writer working with an artist, it's important to learn to write your webcomic in a script format. Like a television or movie screenplay, a comic script gives direction to the artist and tells him what's going on in the panels. Check out comic book writer Dwayne McDuffie's site at http://home-page.mac.com/dmcduffie/site/Scripts.html for some great comic book script examples. See Chapter 8, "The Writing," for more on writing in this format.

Keep in mind that if you're doing a comic strip rather than a comic book for the Web, there may be only a few panels per installment to work with, so your script, if you do one at all, will be only a page or so. Often, a team on a comic strip will just talk things over on the phone or on e-mail, and the artist will go from there.

The drawback to more than one person in a given webcomic enterprise is that one partner is paying the other partners to do the work, eventual profits are split between all, or both. It takes some time for the money from a webcomic to become significant, and dividing up that cookie can make it less of a valuable use of your time.

Finding Talent

You imagine yourself as a great webcomics writer or artist, but you can't do the other thing. Or you can do it all but lettering—your attempt wrecks the whole thing. You want to do a color comic, but you can't even manage MS Paint. It's time to hunt down some talent!

A Fair Exchange

Keep in mind that you will likely need to offer your prospective partner something in return, upfront, to help you out. A promise of future profits somewhere down the line is usually not enough. If your webcomic is intended for a pay collective such as Zuda, you'll have a better chance at finding someone, as you'll just be doing a few comics as a pitch and then doing the actual comic after a pay deal is made.

You can also pay your co-worker out of your own pocket and hope to pay yourself back later with the comic's revenue.

Or you can be incredibly compelling, convince someone to work with you for free, and go from there. Good luck with that—in this business, you get what you pay for. Creators willing to work for nothing are going to give you the type of product that probably won't go very far.

One alternative is to offer a trade. If you need an artist, and you're good at Web design, offer to design some sites in exchange for providing you with art. If you need a writer, and you're good friends with some contacts high up in the comic industry, in exchange for a hook-up, your writer friend can maybe plot and dialogue a few webcomics until you get the hang of it.

Sign On the Dotted Line

It's important to have everyone involved with the comic sign a collaboration agreement. This agreement should spell out exactly what everyone's role is, who's getting paid what, and what percentage creators will receive of profits, merchandising, movie deals, and so on. There is a terrific example of a collaboration agreement at http://www.hollywoodcomics.com/collab.html.

Note that this contract is separate and distinct from any contract you'd sign with a webcomics syndicate or publisher. Also, if you'd like to be sure your contract is airtight (especially if you need to modify it heavily), consult a contract lawyer. You'll have to spend a bit of money for this peace of mind, though.

Stay in Communication

Now that you've found your group, it's important to stay in contact. Get everyone set up on the same instant messenger, whether that is Windows Live Messenger, Yahoo! Messenger, Skype, or some other service. Set up an e-mail group on Yahoo Groups (groups.yahoo.com). Get phone numbers in case of emergency. The nice thing about collaborating on comics in the twenty-first century is that it's absolutely not necessary that creators even live in the same country. Just keep in mind that working hours in the U.S. and the UK are quite different, and it doesn't make sense to demand things by a certain time when that time is five in the morning locally.

The important thing is to communicate. Even if you can't get something done for whatever reason, tell the other people. Work something out. Don't disappear or flake out. If you're going on vacation or you're moving across the country, tell the others. They'll understand.

It's a Commitment

When you've made an agreement with your team to produce a certain amount of work, stick to it. The hardest part about making a webcomic is to do it. Don't get in over your head, but at the same time don't commit to something and then not do it. If your day job or a paid commitment gets in the way, make time to fulfill the webcomic pact that you made with the rest of your team. That's really the concrete on the road to creative and financial success—doing the work, staying committed to the team and the readers, and getting the comic up on the site regularly.

Searching the Web for Talent

Make like Simon Cowell and track down talent at these sites. Just don't make like Simon Cowell and insult them.

www.digitalwebbing.com

This creator's collective site is *the* place to go to find the talent you need. Note that manga-style artists don't usually hang out here, but it's a breeding ground for Western and European-style artists. Either post on the Talent Search forum or use the handy-dandy Talent Search classifieds. Keep in mind that, especially if you mark this as a paid gig, you'll get *a lot* of responses, most of which won't contain the talent you need. Don't take the first one that comes along, and be patient. Ask around and find out about credentials. Your talent has got to be reliable and has to be someone you can trust.

www.deviantart.com

This art-based community site can be overwhelming at first, but skip ahead to the forums and post a classified ad in the Job Offers forum. The forum specifies that the gig must be paid, so be prepared to offer something in return. Also, check the Job Services forum for creators who are looking for work. DeviantArt is the place to go to find artists who draw in the manga style, and many of them are just out of school and are looking for work.

www.penciljack.com

Another site focused on comic book creation, the Help Wanted forum gets a lot of views and is a great place to post your needs. As with the other sites, be sure you are clear, spellcheck your post, and explain exactly what you want. Nothing's worse than getting a flood of e-mails from writers or artists who are all wrong for the project.

www.panelandpixel.com

A fan-created spinoff from comic book creator Warren Ellis's defunct forum, Panel and Pixel is a popular creator-focused forum where anything and everything is discussed—but mostly comics. The Breaking and Entering topic has creator-only sections after your first work is published, but it's also an excellent place to post if you're an artist looking for a writer or a writer looking for an artist.

7

The Webcomics 2.0 Examples

We've talked the talk. Now it's time to show you some webcomics! The following are three webcomics in the humor, adventure, and manga styles.

The Versus Verses

This humor webcomic (see Figure 7.1), written by T Campbell and drawn by Sam Romero, mashes together two rhyming pop-culture elements for comedic effect. *The Versus Verses* makes its debut in the pages of Webcomics 2.0 and will continue in an online venue. Check out Campbell's website at www.webcomics.com for news on *The Versus Verses'* final destination.

The Drifter

This adventure webcomic (see Figure 7.2), written by Steve Horton and drawn by Sam Romero, is a throwback to 1980s detective television shows and stars a hard-bitten detective on the run who goes by the name Kincaid. *The Drifter* makes its debut in the pages of Webcomics 2.0 and will continue as a serial on www.comicspace.com.

Edge the Devilhunter

This manga webcomic (see Figure 7.3), written and drawn by Sam Romero, is a morally ambiguous tale about an assassin of demons in a seedy underworld. This is an original short story in a totally new style. *Edge the Devilhunter*, in its original form, has a large archive on www.graphicsmash.com, and that's where you can follow Edge's continuing adventures.

Figure 7.1 Original pencils of *The Versus Verses* #6.

Figure 7.2 Original pencils of *The Drifter*, Page 1.

Figure 7.3 Original pencils of *Edge the Devilhunter*, Page 1.

The Versus Verses

Cat versus Rat

Potter versus Kotter

Calvin versus Alvin

Rove versus Jove

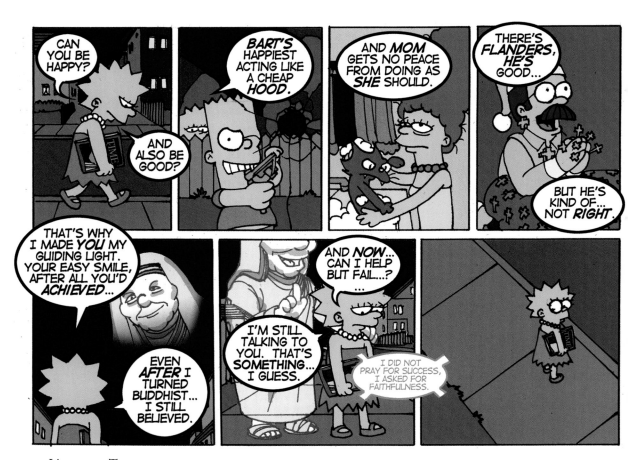

Lisa versus Teresa

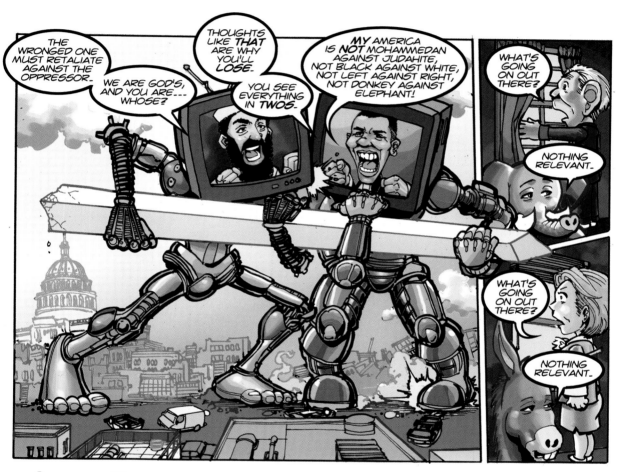

Osama versus Obama

Vader versus Nader

Reagan versus Sagan

The Drifter

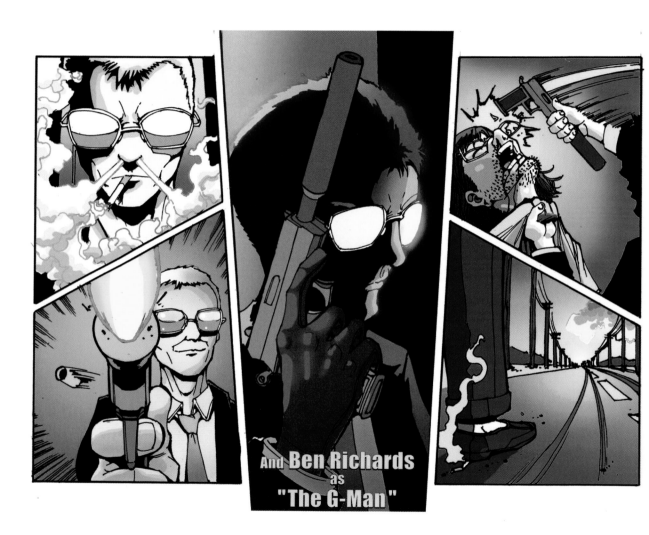

Edge the Devilhunter

8

The Writing

"I can't come up with any ideas."

"I don't have inspiration."

"I have writer's block."

These are all excuses. The act of writing daily is key, whether you're writing for the webcomic, for a novel, or even a blog. Set goals for yourself and set milestones. Start with one page of script per day. One page of script should represent a single installment of your webcomic.

Build up a buffer for yourself so that the artist (if you're not the artist) always has something to do. It usually takes longer to draw a webcomic than it does to write it, so the last thing you want is the artist waiting on your script.

Writing Humor

"Dying is easy; comedy is hard," said Sir Donald Wolfit, purportedly as his last words. Humor writing is a tricky subject. It can be tough to make something funny. Often, we throw whatever we can at the webcomics wall and see what sticks. A funny situation or joke you've observed may or may not translate well into a webcomic; you won't know until you try. Then again, simply having your characters be themselves in the face of a specific situation can often lead to humor.

The first thing to decide is what type of humor you're going for. See Chapter 2, "Humor," for several examples of popular humor subjects in webcomics, including video games, science fiction, autobiography, and pop culture. Another good subject is political humor. Political webcomics hearken back to the master political cartoonists of old, successfully skewering politicians for a laugh and a message.

Often, the key to making these mundane situations funny is finding something ridiculous about them.

If your interest lies in laughing at something else, give it a try. You just may come at it from a unique perspective that people might find refreshing.

The Character Bible

When launching a brand-new webcomic, one of the first things to develop is a character bible. This document not only helps you understand your characters better and gives them three dimensions, it also assists the artist with the initial character sketches.

The character bible should list each important character that the story will introduce. If you plan to introduce more characters later down the line, that's OK. It's up to you whether or not to list them—you may not quite yet have a handle on those future characters. The important thing is to write about who will be the initial focus of the story.

Describe the character's looks, personality, and motivation. Feel free to reveal all the secrets that your work contains, because nobody will see it except you and the artist. It may be adapted later into a section of the website, but the spoilers will be removed.

Character Bible: The Drifter

Pete Kincaid

Pete Kincaid has longish brown hair and wears brown or gray suits, as was common in the 1980s, with the tie undone. He's got a weathered but kind face.

Formerly very happy in his growing New Jersey detective agency, The Drifter has undergone a radical personality shift ever since being forced to hit the road. He's nihilistic—almost suicidal, as he believes his life is unusually finite. Someday soon, the G-Man will catch up with Pete and kill him. He wants to help as many people as he can, but being forced to run so often means that his help must come fast and therefore can be riddled with mistakes.

His feelings for his assistant, Jennifer, are "complicated." Though he's outspoken about their relationship as a strict partnership, in his heart he's beginning to feel differently.

Jennifer Lancaster

A beautiful brunette with a razor-sharp mind but a clumsy way about her, Jennifer Lancaster calls herself Pete Kincaid's business partner, though Pete refers to her as his "assistant." It's this dichotomy that drives her to succeed and make up for Pete's mistakes.

The biggest of these mistakes, in Jen's mind, is Pete being resigned to his fate at the hands of the G-Man. Jennifer has secretly taken steps to ensure that when Pete can't run anymore, he'll survive his encounter. After that, her plan is to take the fight to the G-Men themselves and get them off the back of Kincaid & Lancaster once and for all. Then, maybe, they can settle down in a practice somewhere, and maybe Jen can finally admit how she feels about Pete. But not before.

The G-Man

The G-Man is a criminal boss of a shadowy organization, all of whose members wear reflective glasses, stay in the shadows, and look like him. A case that Pete Kincaid took on recently forced him to cross paths with the G-Man, and things went badly. Ever since, the G-Man has been obsessed with finding Pete and killing him, going so far as to make this hit the group's primary purpose. The G-Man is a nasty piece of work.

The Comic Script

When working as part of a creative team, it's important to standardize communication between the writer and artist. Most teams in comics have used the comic script format to do so.

Comic scripts are related but not identical to scripts used in the television and movie industries. One big difference that people should realize, whether coming in from those industries or not, is the concept of static panels.

Within a single comic panel, only one movement or action per object can occur. In other words, it's impossible for someone to move across the room and pick up an object in one panel. It takes a panel to move and a panel to pick up. Better yet, chuck the moving and just have the guy pick up the object.

Another tip is to limit one-panel installments, also called splash pages. These should be saved for key moments.

Lastly, a comic strip has one to five panels, and a comic page usually has no more than six or seven panels. Panels tend to increase during a fast, intense sequence of events and decrease when the reader is meant to pause on a singular moment.

If you're going solo, rather than as part of a team, it still helps to learn this format. It might help you get your thoughts on paper before the drawing starts.

Script Glossary

Caption
A squarish box containing lettering, as opposed to a balloon. A caption is where narration and thoughts can go or information about the time or place of the scene.

Close On
When you tell an artist to *close on* something, that means he should get closer to an object that was already present in a previous panel.

Cut To
This simply means that the visual changes from one spot to another spot in the same scene.

Establishing Shot

We don't use this term in this script specifically, but it's still important to know. When starting a new scene in a new location, it often helps to begin with an establishing shot, which is a shot of the exterior of the place where the scene is taking place. Sometimes it's the city, sometimes it's a building, sometimes it's a car. Sometimes it's none of the above. The important thing here is that the establishing shot is the setting of the current scene.

Frame

Often the writer will instruct the artist to frame a shot a certain way, meaning that the camera should be zoomed in or zoomed out to make an object more or less visible.

Logo

The logo is a stylized font representing your webcomic, and you may want it to appear in the body of an early installment for effect. The logo will be used primarily on the website and on merchandise.

Panel

Most scripts have a panel-by-panel breakdown of the events on a specific page or installment. Begin with Panel 1 and move to the last panel on the page, in the order that the page is meant to be read.

Point of View

Point of view, sometimes abbreviated POV, is where the "camera" is placed in a scene. If you write from a specific character's POV, then we see what that character sees. A POV can also be from high-up (*bird's eye view*) or way down (*snail's eye view*). Just beware when referring to a *helicopter shot*; we heard of one artist who misunderstood and drew a helicopter!

Reference

It helps to give an artist reference for any real-world objects that you're asking him to draw. Images.google.com is a great place, but make sure the artist doesn't just copy what is likely a copyrighted photo. Tell the artist to use the photo as a starting point, just to be sure the details are correct.

SFX

Short for sound effects, these are what the letterer or artist draws that represent sounds. Some webcomics use SFX only for big sounds; some, especially manga, put SFX everywhere.

The Drifter: Script

Here's the script for the entire 10-page *Drifter* short story at the center of this book. Feel free to refer back and forth between the art and the script. You can see that artist Sam Romero followed the script closely in some spots and made changes in other spots, but all for the better.

Page 1

The Drifter's car is a 1980 Chevrolet Camaro Z28. Here's some reference:

Exterior:
http://www.nastyz28.com/forum/gallery/showgallery.php/cat/511

Interior:
http://www.nastyz28.com/forum/gallery/showphoto.php/photo/2887/cat/511,

http://www.nastyz28.com/forum/gallery/showphoto.php/photo/2486/cat/511

Panel 1: A closeup of the speedometer.

Panel 2: A closeup of The Drifter's hand as he changes the gear shift.

Panel 3: The car leaping through the panel, perhaps over something!

Page 2

Panel 1: The car hits the ground.

Panel 2: Close in on The Assistant in the passenger seat and The Drifter in the driver's seat, jerking the wheel hard in one direction as the car peels to a stop!

Panel 3: The Drifter in the driver's seat and The Assistant in the passenger seat, both with adrenaline pumping, looking in the distance to make sure they lost 'em. This panel's going to have lettering superimposed over it, so keep that in mind.

LOGO: THE DRIFTER

Page 3

Here's some reference for The Drifter's gun:

Drifter gun choices

Colt 1911 chambered in .45ACP:
http://images.google.com/images?gbv=2&svnum=10&hl=en&safe=off&q=colt+1911+acp&btnG=Search+Images

Large-frame Ruger double-action:
http://images.google.com/images?gbv=2&svnum=10&hl=en&safe=off&q=ruger+p85&btnG=Search+Images

Center panel (tall): Action shot of The Drifter with weapon drawn.

CAPTION: Starring Peter Kincaid.

Panel 1 (upper left): A closeup of The Drifter smacking a clip into his gun.

Panel 2 (upper right): The Drifter punching some guy out with a haymaker.

Panel 3 (lower left): The Drifter on a phone stand—not a phone booth. Close in so we can see him on the phone. Reference for that: http://www.supermanhomepage.com/images/phonebooth/movie-phonebooth.jpg

Panel 4 (lower right): The Drifter looking behind him at a woman walking past in a tight dress.

Page 4

Some reference for The Assistant's gun (also The Drifter's backup weapon):

S&W 620 in .38: http://www.gunblast.com/SW619-620.htm.

Center panel (tall): Action shot of The Assistant, also with weapon drawn.

CAPTION: Also Starring Jennifer Lancaster.

Panel 1 (upper left): The Assistant has on a slinky dress and is pretending to be a lounge singer in a seedy bar. The Drifter is enjoying himself in the audience.

Panel 2 (upper right): The Assistant is crouched in her normal clothes with both hands on the gun, shooting something or someone out of frame.

Panel 3 (lower left): The Assistant slapping another woman hard, in the face.

Panel 4 (lower right): The Assistant with a flashlight, lifting out a manila file folder in a file cabinet

Page 5

G-Man gun choices

Browning Hi-Power 9mm double-stack (15 rounds): http://www.back-countryjournal.com/P8110032.jpg; http://www.browning.com/products/catalog/firearms/detail.asp?value=007b&cat_id=051&type_id=003.

Center panel (tall): The G-Man in the shadows, gun drawn.

CAPTION: And Ben Richards as "The G-Man"

Panel 1 (upper left): The G-Man smoking a cigarette in the shadows. A lot of smoke here.

Panel 2 (upper right): The G-Man clobbers a guy by pistol-whipping him.

Panel 3 (lower left): The G-Man is shooting into the frame with a silencer.

Panel 4 (lower right): The G-Man crushes a cigarette butt with his heel, and in the road we can see black burned-rubber tire tracks.

Page 6

Tall center panel is a tall and large Pakistani individual. This is our guest star for this week's episode.

The point of view for this panel should be low, looking up. Snail's eye view? He should have a white tank top and jeans. He should be tattooed, like so. Pick one of these, whichever won't give you nightmares to draw.

http://en.wikipedia.org/wiki/Mehndi

http://pakpics.wordpress.com/category/mehndi-designs-tattoos/

Upper left panel: The Pakistani in a pinstriped business suit, arms folded. He looks like a bodyguard or bouncer.

Upper right panel: The Pakistani swings a baseball bat straight through the windshield of a 1980s car! A different model than The Drifter's. Doesn't matter what. Glass is flying everywhere.

Lower left panel: The Pakistani is lifting some poor fool off the ground by his collar.

Lower right panel: Close up of The Pakistani with one fist in the other palm, cracking the knuckles of his fist. Does that make sense?

CAPTION: Special Guest Star, Rahim Malik as "The Pakistani"

Page 7

Splash: High overhead shot of a busy highway, with multiple lanes in each direction. The highway should go from bottom left to upper right, or bottom right to upper left, in a straight line.

In the lane just right of center going north is our hero's Camaro with both The Drifter and The Assistant in it.

Frame the car so that we can tell it's our guys, even though we're pretty high up.

CAPTION: My name is KINCAID. I'm a DETECTIVE.

CAPTION: I had a comfortable PRIVATE PRACTICE in New Brunswick.

CAPTION: Until I took on the wrong CLIENT—pissed off the wrong PEOPLE.

Page 8

Panel 1: This is inside Kincaid's office. The door to his office has glass windows and has his name written on it in bold black lettering, but on the outside so we see it in reverse. Think the old TV show *Barney Miller*. Here's an example in the background: http://www.tvguide.com/images/pgimg/barney-miller.jpg.

The glass is in the process of being elbowed in, and glass is shattering everywhere, but we should still be able to read KINCAID somehow. Maybe shatter it in order from left to right, like The Spirit would do?

CAPTION: If it wasn't for LANCASTER—my ASSISTANT—who watched the whole thing go down—

Panel 2: Close on the newly created hole in the glass. The G-Man is peeking through.

CAPTION: I'd be DEAD ALREADY.

Panel 3: Now, the G-Man and several G-Men (who look similar to each other, but dress totally different from the G-Man) are inside the room. We're getting an establishing shot of the whole office from their point of view. Their guns are drawn.

The office should have a secretary's desk near the door and a closed-off secondary room where Kincaid actually works. There should be file cabinets behind the secretary's desk and windows on the walls. The door to the secondary room is open just a tiny crack. It opens inward.

Page 9

Panel 1: Cut to Lancaster, The Assistant, who's inside the inner office. Her back is to the cracked door, and she's got her gun drawn and pointed upward. She's listening, and she looks like she's trying to keep her composure but is pretty freaked out.

Panel 2: Close on the inner door—Lancaster accidentally bumps it, and it latches closed!

SFX: CLICK!

Panel 3: The G-Men open fire on the door and shoot it full of holes!

Panel 4: Cut to inside the inner office, where the G-Men are pushing the ruined door out of the way, but there's nobody there. The window is open, though.

Panel 5: Cut to outside that window at street level. There's a fire escape that stops a few feet from the ground, and I need the moment where Lancaster drops to the street in a crouch, looking upward for a moment.

Page 10

Panel 1: Back to the highway—the present day, but a closer view than on page 7. The Camaro is taking an exit on the right side.

CAPTION: The only way I'm staying AHEAD is if I keep MOVING.

Panel 2: Close on Kincaid and Lancaster. Kincaid is turning the wheel to his right. They both have determined expressions.

CAPTION: So I have to RUN.

CAPTION: Someday SOON I'll stop running, turn around, and fight back.

CAPTION: That day will be the day I DIE.

Panel 3: Closer on just Kincaid.

CAPTION: Until then...

CAPTION: I'm going to help as many people as I CAN.

CAPTION: CONTINUED on www.comicspace.com!

Writing Structure

Unlike a print comic book or graphic novel, webcomics have no finite page count. Your beginning, middle, and end need not fit between the staples of a 22-page comic book. You don't need to write a story that's exactly six issues in length to fit into a trade paperback. This freedom from rigid page counts, though, means that you have to be twice as aware of story structure. Just because your installment or page count is open ended doesn't mean your story shouldn't go somewhere.

Two Approaches

There are two major approaches to storytelling. You can base it on the characters and their personalities, reactions, interactions, and quirks. The actual events that happen to the characters are important insofar as they give you more emotion and personality to play with. This sort of approach is called *character driven*.

The second approach is to have an overall plot, such as a quest, and have events move inexorably forward. The story is the thing. The characters, while important, are there to serve the sequence of events. This is called *story driven*.

Many quality stories cherry-pick from the best elements of both approaches, but there are excellent stories that are primarily one or the other. Whatever feels like the most natural approach for your story is the one you should go with.

Still another approach is to throw story and character out the window and just tell good jokes. This is the gag-a-day webcomic.

The Story Arc

A story arc is a sequence of events told from the beginning to the end. Story arcs often come in layers. Your webcomic may have one huge over-arching story arc. Perhaps you have someplace in mind you want your characters to get, years from now. You know what their death scenes look like, and you want to get a chance to write those scenes someday. You know for a fact that two characters will hook up, but you want to take your sweet time getting there.

You may not have a longer arc in mind. You're more interested in telling a series of stories until you run out of ideas, which may be never. That's perfectly all right, because what we're more concerned with are the shorter story arcs within that epic. These arcs represent the situations that your characters are in right now. Here's how they solve, or fail to solve, their current problems, and here's how the story alters their lives, if at all. These arcs can last one installment (though that'd be kind of tricky) and can take as long as weeks or months or years to complete.

The former "longer arc" approach can be compared to the *Lord of the Rings* books or movies, where there is one complete story to tell. The series of stories, or episodic approach, can be compared to the James Bond movies. Every movie is a fresh start and a new adventure for Bond.

Gag-a-Day

Another note on the gag-a-day format. Gag-based strips represent a huge percentage of what's popular on the Web. Many of these webcomics don't have story arcs; some of them do. Some of them kill off main characters only to bring them back to life next time. There are no rules to comedy, so when writing a gag comic, feel free to ignore arcs altogether.

Three Act Structure

Regardless of how many installments belong in your story arc, it's a good idea to structure the arc so that it follows three acts. You may already be doing this unconsciously. Most fiction is written in three acts. Those that aren't tend to meander and leave readers feeling oddly unsatisfied.

Act One: The Problem

In the first act, a problem, conflict, or goal is introduced to the characters. This is something that will be resolved by the end of the arc. This stumbling block is the heart of the story you're telling and is one big reason the story's being told in the first place.

Don't start the story arc at the beginning. Yes, that's right. Act One should start as deep into the events as possible. This technique is called *in media res*. By dispensing with all the boring stuff that happens before the real meat of the story, readers are immediately pulled in. If there's any important backstory, the readers will be filled in as they go.

If this is the very first story arc of the webcomic, this is also where the characters are introduced.

Don't begin with the characters' origins, either, to use a word from super-hero comics. Revealing the characters' backstories here will only delay the start of the story. Instead, the origin can be revealed over the course of the story where necessary, if you choose to reveal it at all.

Act Two: The Complication

In the second act, things go wrong. Obstacles are placed in the path of our protagonist. The hero's life is in danger, or he has lost it all in pursuit of the goal. This is the part where you can't be afraid to let bad things happen if it serves the story and doesn't wreck the characters in the process.

Try to write Act Two as if the reader will have little idea how things will get fixed. In other words, make it seem as if there is no solution or no way out, unless the reader is exceptionally clever and guesses what is going on. Make things really bad for the heroes. Some writers sum up Act Two with three words: "Things get worse."

Act Two should have a major dramatic or compelling moment, but not the biggest one. Save that for Act Three.

Act Three: The Turning Point

Act Three is where the protagonist rises above being beaten down in Act Two. This turning point leads to the climax of the story, involving the most dramatic moment of the story arc. The climax is where some sort or triumph or epiphany takes place. The characters affected by the story grow and change in some way. The quest is solved or at least advanced further for the next story arc to pick up. The arc's conflict is resolved, but not always favorably or in a way the characters expect.

Following the climax, at the end of the arc, is a period of relief called a *denouement*. Think about the end of an action movie, where there are fire trucks and police cars, the main character kisses the love interest and punches the unfairly belligerent FBI agent, and the camera slowly pulls away to a bird's eye view.

Or think about the end of many of the *Harry Potter* novels, where Harry sits down with Professor Dumbledore. The professor explains to a bewildered Harry what just happened during the story's climax.

The basic problem/complication/turning point structure can be messed with a bit, but like any such rules, it helps to master them first so that you know what you're breaking. In the end, most writers fall back on the three act structure because it works.

Rising Action

When writing a dramatic webcomic, within a specific story arc it's important to consider the concept of rising action. Each of the key scenes or "beats" in your story arc should generally be more important than the last. That is, begin the arc with smaller drama. Save your second most dramatic scene for the middle of the arc, during Act Two, and your most dramatic scene for the end of Act Three. By not dropping the bomb too early, you ensure that people come back for more.

Subplots

While your main story is progressing, you may want to have subplots involving one or more of the supporting cast members. The main plot, then, is called the A Plot, while the subplot is called the B Plot. These subplots can have arcs that run exactly parallel to the main story arc, but most writers have found that it's more interesting to stagger them. In other words, when things start getting really bad for the main characters in Act Two, cut away for a moment and introduce a new situation involving supporting cast members. Or during Act Three, when things resolve for the A Plot, things get worse for the B Plot. Some A Plots and B Plots run entirely parallel and may share certain themes but don't intersect. Some plots eventually join together and reach a combined resolution. It depends on the story.

It's also common for a B Plot to take over the story completely, if it has just started to get underway as the original A Plot is finishing up. The point at which the B Plot takes over is where a new story arc begins.

Some writers like to introduce the next arc at the very end of the previous arc, as a sort of preview. This is less a case of a B Plot taking over and more of giving the reader a hook to keep reading after the denouement.

It's also the case that a B plot can be long-term and can run for ages while multiple A plots come and go. Perhaps this long-running B plot finally ties into the main story, but not until the end of Act Three.

Flashbacks

A flashback is a look into the past relative to the present day of the webcomic. It's often a way to give meaning to present-day actions by relating them to past actions. It can give justification for a decision made by a character. It also allows development of characters who may not be alive or around in the present day.

Due to the daily or weekly narrative of most webcomics, an extended flashback sequence featuring characters in earlier incarnations can be problematic. New readers may be thrown off and think that this situation is the status quo. It also presents a problem to you, the writer: You may find the past too interesting to leave.

Some fiction writers abhor flashbacks in general. Stephen King almost never uses them, preferring to start at the beginning and reveal the past through present-day actions.

In manga, flashbacks are common. Often whole story arcs or even volumes are devoted to them.

If you do decide to use this technique, be sure to have the artist do something to the panels to make it obvious. Putting clouds or a design around the panels, making the panel borders white with black outlines, or putting an explanatory caption in each installment's Panel 1 are all valid approaches.

If you find yourself enjoying a trip to the past, consider using it as a springboard to a new prequel series. Though running two or more webcomics at the same time is challenging, the fans may relish the opportunity to get to know characters even better.

Transitioning from One Webcomic to Another

During the course of your webcomics' life, you may find the story drawing to a close. You still love webcomics and still want to do them, but your current webcomic is coming to a sort of natural conclusion. Or you may have intended it to be a finite series all along.

Creating a new webcomic and keeping the old audience is a challenge. The fans may have so much emotion invested in the old webcomic that they rebel against something new from the same creators.

As in other fiction, if the new series is a continuation of the old series, you may have an easier time holding on to readers. Retaining the original creative team on the new project is also a benefit.

You may also be loath to pull the plug if you've spent money on merchandise, convention banners, and so on (see Chapter 11, "Promotion"). You'll have a hard time getting rid of the rest of your stuff with just the archives and no new installments.

Ultimately, though, webcomics creators create for themselves and not for an audience or a T-shirt. Your new series may end up being just as creatively and financially rewarding as the old, if not more so.

This brings up another point. Many creators try something new, if their old one just didn't catch on, despite their best efforts. In this case, it may be wise to wrap it up and make something different. Don't give up, though, unless you really have tried everything.

All Write Now

Writing and art go hand-in-hand to create the ultimate webcomic. Neither is more important than the other; rather, they share responsibility for victory or defeat. Writing webcomics well, avoiding clichés, and making things funny or interesting takes a lot of practice, but well-written webcomics can be extremely rewarding. It's said that fans come for the art, but they stay for the writing.

The Webcomics 2.0 Interview: *Inverloch* and *The Phoenix Requiem*

Sarah Ellerton is the mastermind behind one of the most popular fantasy webcomics on the entire Web—*Inverloch* (inverloch.seraph-inn.com). Originally conceived and followed through as a finite story, this webcomic, which ended in mid-2007, had nearly 200,000 pageviews per day. It was replaced by another fantasy webcomic, called *The Phoenix Requiem* (requiem.seraph-inn.com), which is about as different from *Inverloch* as it can be and still be fantasy. Ellerton offers some tips about transitioning from a popular but finite series to another.

Webcomics 2.0: Tell me a little bit about *Inverloch* and why it came to an end.

Sarah Ellerton: I wrote *Inverloch* with the intention of it being a complete, finite story, much like a traditional novel. The script was written before I made a start on the drawn pages, although it was edited and improved as I went along. The majority of webcomics are ongoing serials; I really wanted to do something different, even if it meant an inevitable end.

WC20: You're transitioning directly into *The Phoenix Requiem*. Is this new comic related at all to *Inverloch*? Tell me a little bit about it.

SE: *The Phoenix Requiem* has no association with *Inverloch*; it is a new story, with new characters, set in a different world. Like *Inverloch*, it will also be a fixed length with a defined beginning, middle, and end. It's also a fantasy story, but is set in an era modeled after Victorian England and focuses more on the supernatural with elements of horror rather than a typical swords and sorcery fable.

WC20: Do you have any advice about carrying over readership from an ending comic to a new one? What if people are really upset that their favorite characters are going away?

SE: I can understand how people must feel about seeing the end of their favorite characters; I must also admit to being sad about the thought of not drawing or writing about them again. The readers and I have all spent up to three years following their journey, so it can be difficult to leave them behind. However, I look at it as a challenge, to create a new set of characters that are different from those I have made in the past, yet still interesting and likable.

As far as story goes, I'm trying to make it my goal to write something that will appeal to the readership I have, while also trying to draw in a new kind of audience. The story is a little more mature and a little darker.

WC20: Is there anything you'll be able to do with *The Phoenix Requiem* that you weren't able to do with *Inverloch*?

SE: Since I'm writing a darker, less fantastical story, it's allowing me to explore some more adult themes that I wouldn't have been able to incorporate into *Inverloch*. Of course I have to be careful about alienating my younger readers, but I hope they will still find much to enjoy.

WC20: What other projects are you working on?

SE: Unfortunately, my full-time job prevents me from being able to take on too much at once, even though I have plenty of ideas tumbling around in my head.

9

The Art

Artists on some of the world's most popular webcomics began life with talent that was not apparent. In the print or newspaper comics world, this might have meant these webcomics would never have had a chance. Online, though, these webcomics artists kept at it. They hammered away at their craft until it got better. The progression is visible in real time through the archives. Simply practicing on a regular schedule over and over was enough to improve.

Webcomics Art Dos and Don'ts

Here are some dos and don'ts for the beginning webcomics artist.

- Don't leave eraser marks or smudges on the pencil art.
- Do use good quality paper from Bristol or another top brand.
- Don't use printer paper. You might as well be drawing on the back of an envelope.
- Do ink with a quality ink pen, brush, or marker. Don't use a Bic pen or a Magic Marker.
- Do leave room for lettering. Don't crowd the entire panel with the characters and setting.
- Do use a quality Wacom graphics tablet or mouse when working digitally.
- Do strike a proper balance between paper-and-pencil work and digital work.

You can go that route if you feel your skills are not up to par and you feel your fans will stick with you as your art evolves. If your rendering isn't where you'd like it to be, you still need to ensure your art is clean. Don't hamstring yourself.

Drawing a Webcomic: Step by Step

Here's the process that many webcomics artists use, from the blank page to the scanned, finished art. Also, check the sidebar for several important tips from the artist on this book, Sam Romero.

The Webcomics 2.0 Interview: Sam Romero

Sam Romero, the artist on *Webcomics 2.0*, got his start drawing the Graphic Smash webcomic *Edge the Devilhunter* (www.graphicsmash.com/comics/edgethedevilhunter.php). Since then, he's drawn, colored, and lettered dozens of illustrations for this book and drawn the webcomic *The Versus Verses* for T Campbell. After that, he drew a *Gambling Souls* short story for the mobile webcomic collective Clickwheel, with Steve Horton (the author of this book).

Romero's learned a lot over his freelance art career, and here are some tips he's picked up along the way.

Webcomics 2.0: What are some ways an artist can improve his drawing ability?

Sam Romero: First would be to get in the habit of doodling and practicing to draw what you see. Gaining the ability to draw what you see is the first step toward better drawing, training your eyes to copy what you observe. I started learning how to draw copying covers from X-men comics.

Then the next step from observation is knowledge of objects and space. In a way, it's sort of learning to see things as three-dimensional. Hence, a lot of art instructional [books] refer to the basic shapes and where they appear in nature. Sooner or later, after enough practice, you can look at something and break it down in your head. And that eventually translates into what you draw. I know this probably sounds weird, but it's, in effect, training your mind to see differently.

The next step is regimentation. With the ability to break down objects in your mind, now you have to learn how objects are constructed in relation to each other. Things like drawing the human head or a body in head lengths, how something is constructed in nature—you'll have to basically learn how to reproduce that by memory. After a while, that becomes second nature. A body is around six and a half head lengths long, the eyes fall in halfway on the head, etc. Anyone who's picked up "how-tos" before knows what I'm talking about.

The very last step is the most fun and rewarding part, which is free experimentation. Now that you know the rules of drawing off the top of your head, you can break them and find out how others break 'em. Throughout your life, you'll be continually modifying what you know and discovering new ways to implement your techniques. This is where studying your own work and *especially* that of other artists [is important]. You have to know who's out there and what they're doing. What they do better, what they don't do better. And that's where you eventually develop your style.

This is a process that doesn't happen overnight. Depending on your skill level, it might take years. My art teachers all told me I had natural talent, but it took me *years* to develop my current level of skill. And I'm still checking other artists out and reviewing what I know about drawing.

WC20: Tell me about the importance of proper tools and paper to the artist.

SR: A common misconception among starting artists, and I had them a lot when I started out, is how big a deal your tools are. Well-functioning equipment is important, no doubt, but what matters the most is your ability to work with the tools you have. Sometimes starting artists work against their tools, and it usually ends up with bad results. Make sure you have the right equipment, make sure it's functioning right, and make sure your drawing surface is clean, smooth, and of the proper weight, if the art's ink-heavy. But don't always blame your tools for bad results. I can produce pretty good results with a sharpie as I would a g-pen. Again, it all depends on your knowledge of the tools you're using.

WC20: How can an artist improve faces and facial expressions, and how important is that to the overall package?

SR: This, again, goes back to what I talked about when observing objects in nature. Learn how your face changes when in certain moods. See how an eye is constructed, how it works, and play around with the parts. Facial expressions are the most crucial element in portraying human emotion, so having them down pat is pretty important. It helps to think of how the face expresses itself by breaking it down into two sections: the eye section and the mouth section. The eye section includes the eyes, of course, and the brow. The mouth section includes the mouth and the chin. The eye section is the most important part. Pretty much any artist will tell you that. You can push a lot of ideas with the right set of eyes on a character, even contradictory ones, like sharp eyes on a good character, innocent eyes on an evil character, or lazy eyes on a nimble character.

Depending on the expression you want to represent, you have to have those sections working in conjunction to provide the right effect. For beginning artists, it shouldn't be entirely difficult to mold both according to your dramatic needs. For the eyes, the only parts that really move are the upper lid folds and the brow muscles; for the mouth area, the periphery of the mouth and the jaw if the mouth opens wide. How you combine their movements is up for you to observe how they work in nature—shelve the knowledge in your mind, and reproduce it on paper.

WC20: When working solo, how important is it to script the story first? Do you find yourself just drawing from the head? Do you do outlines or other organizing efforts first?

SR: Well, when I first started out, I came up with the script as I went. I had good ideas, but I ended up not organizing and refining them well and pretty much throwing all I had at the audience. Sucks to be a noob. The results, while okay, were convoluted and nowhere near clean and professional. For any artist wanting to write his own material, learn how to write! It's an entirely different discipline, and with comics, there's an extra challenge in balancing imagery with words. Since there are constraints on how much time you can spend planning and creating webcomics, if you're both drawing and writing the thing, it's crucial to start with some prewriting and work from there toward creating a general plot and outline for the story that you can work from. Write down some dialogue that you want to include and work it in where appropriate. Cut stuff that isn't all that important or that you can introduce later in the storyline. All the pieces matter. Also, make sure you know the minds of your characters! Soon enough you'll start noticing them become flesh and blood, going in their own directions, and producing strange and pleasing results within your story. Don't restrain your characters with what you want to do. You might be God, but they have free will.

WC20: When working with a writer, how do you know when to follow the script and when to make changes for the better?

SR: I try to stay as faithful as I can to a writer's script. Being an artist, you must respect a collaborator's vision. But sometimes, when your vision comes into conflict with the other person's vision, go ahead and negotiate. Bounce the ideas back and forth. If your gut tells you this sucks or this is lame, go chew it out with your writer. But be friends in the end. It's nothing personal. The quality of the work itself is what's paramount in the end, not your respective egos. And there are plenty of those out there.

Thumbnails

You may elect to begin by sketching out several quick thumbnails, or small, sketchy panels on a separate piece of paper. These thumbnails suggest camera angles and character placements and may be invaluable when actually drawing the webcomic.

Study the Script

If you're strictly an artist and are not writing the webcomic, it'd be wise to refer to The Comic Script section of Chapter 8, "The Writing." When working with a writer early in your creative relationship, it's a good idea to spend some time discussing the early scripts. Make sure the scripts make sense and make sure the writer is scripting to your comfort level. For example, the writer may not be putting in enough detail or [may be] including too much extraneous information. Or the writer may not be introducing objects important to the story early enough.

This communication is important and is preferable to just deviating from the script without talking it over. As the artist, you may have better ideas about layout and camera angles. Bring them up in an e-mail, and, odds are, the writer will be OK with the changes. Later on in your partnership, the writer may become more comfortable with you making the necessary changes where you see fit. Similarly, you may find the script design altering to suit your style. This synergy almost invariably produces better webcomics.

The Panel Borders

Your webcomic installment may have the same number of panels every time, or the panel count may vary according to the script or the needs of the story. Determine the size and quantity of panels in your installment and ink them using a pen or marker and straight edge on paper or using the shape tools in Photoshop or the panel creation tool in Manga Studio, if on the computer. Figure 9.1 is an example of a page with the panels drawn in.

Pencils Out

Now it's time to start drawing. Some artists do a low-level drawing across the entire installment first. Some complete an entire single panel at a time. Some work from the background in, and some work from the faces out. There's no one right method, but there may be a better method for you than what you're doing. Try different approaches and see what really helps you get the art finished.

Some artists will actually sketch in where they want the speech balloons to go, though your letterer, if you have one, may want to handle balloon placement. Either way, remember to leave room for dialogue and captions.

Sam Romero's *Edge the Devilhunter* starts to take shape in the pencil stage (Figure 9.2).

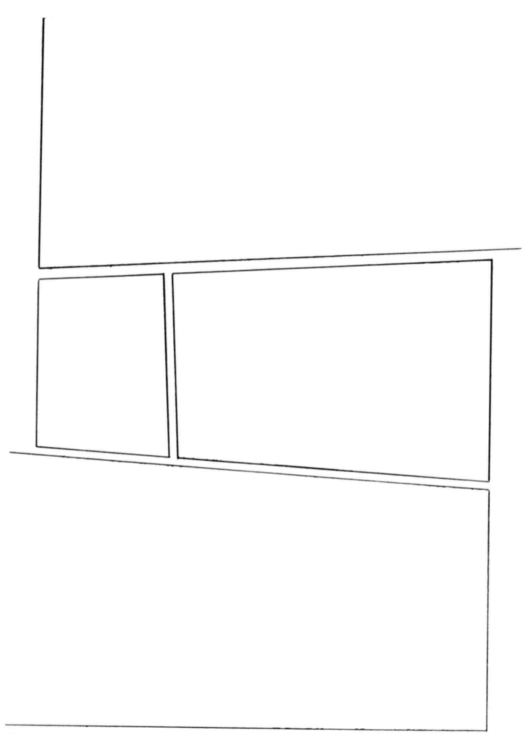

Figure 9.1 Artist Sam Romero begins by drawing in the panels.

Figure 9.2 Romero then pencils in the installment using .05 mechanical pencils. Since he's inking it himself, he doesn't need to get too detailed.

Iced Ink

Using a pen, brush, or marker of your choice, ink in the pencils, apply black to areas that need it, and give elements line weight and definition. Then erase the pencils with a good professional eraser, not the one on the back of the pencil. *Edge the Devilhunter* now has form and definition (Figure 9.3).

Many creators scan in the work at this step and then finish the art on the computer. Some prefer to use the computer just for lettering, and some do the entire thing old school—no computer aspect at all until it's done.

Scanning It In

Many artists scan in the work at this step, but you may elect to scan earlier or later. Either way, you'll need to invest in a scanner large enough for the paper you're working on. If you're drawing on 8.5 × 11, any scanner will do; otherwise, you'll need an 11 × 17 scanner, which you can find online for a few hundred bucks.

Black and white, unfinished art should be scanned in at 300 to 400 dpi, and either black-and-white or grayscale. Black-and-white scans are for clean, well-inked pieces with little shading. Grayscale scans are for the heavily shaded work, or if you want to scan pencils in. If you've somehow colored your work on paper, then scan in color.

After importing the scanned file into your favorite graphics software, it's important to then adjust the levels. In Photoshop, you'll want to go to Adjust > Levels. Select the darkest part of your drawing with the black dropper and the lightest part of your drawing with the white dropper. Also, adjust the brightness and contrast as desired.

If you scanned in as grayscale, try changing the mode to a black-and-white drawing, and see how it looks. After that, turn it back to grayscale. If you plan to color it, select the RGB or CMYK color space at this time. See the "Coloring Webcomics Effectively" sidebar for more tips on which color space you should be choosing.

Figure 9.3 Romero inks the drawing. Among his tools are a Windsor-Newton Series 7 no. 2 brush for thick lines and a g-pen with a Tachikawa pen holder for the remaining linework.

Finished Art

After the art is scanned in, the work is then sometimes toned or colored. Black-and-white webcomics can be finished by the inking step if enough shading is applied. Manga and many Western-style webcomics are not shaded in the inking step; instead, a series of tones or shades are applied. These tones give the work a three-dimensional quality. The best program for applying tones is Manga Studio, in either Debut or EX flavor. The full EX version has more tones to choose from. However, artist Sam Romero used Photoshop, which works nearly as well (Figure 9.4).

Color

You may choose to color the work instead. Photoshop is the weapon of choice here. If you color your webcomic periodically, or want to, remember that coloring is an entirely different art than penciling and inking. Study books on color theory. Color on one or more layers in Photoshop separate from the line art. Make sure you save the black-and-white version as a separate file.

The Webcomics 2.0 Interview: Coloring Webcomics Effectively

Why live in a black-and-white world forever? It helps to spice up the occasional webcomics installment with color. There's an art to coloring webcomics, and it's far different from the pencil and ink process.

We asked Ian Sokoliwski, professional comics illustrator and colorist (www.ianthecomicartist.com) for some tips for new webcomics colorists.

Webcomics 2.0: What are some basic coloring tips for a new webcomics creator?

Ian Sokoliwski: Most coloring tips that would apply for print comics apply equally well to webcomics—make either the foregrounds or the backgrounds saturated but not both, allowing the characters/places to separate being a big one. Treat the webcomic as any other piece of art, paying attention to consistent light sources.

By saturated, I mean dark, intense, or both. A light shade of blue is much less saturated than a very dark shade of blue, for example.

Figure 9.4 Romero has chosen to use manga-style tones rather than color for *Edge the Devilhunter.*

WC20: What are some basic things to avoid?

IS: If you are coloring the lineart of another artist, don't fight that lineart. If the original lineart indicates the lighting is coming from a particular direction, then let the coloring do the same. Remember that your job is to help and enhance the storytelling, not to fight it.

Generally, the lineart itself should indicate where the light is coming from. The easiest way to determine this is by looking at the nose on most characters. If the shadow under the nose falls to the left, that means the light is coming from the right. So the coloring will be lighter on the right side of the face than on the left side, as more light is hitting that side.

Also—and this is really, really important—try and stay away from making your colors too muddy and too similar to each other. One thing about webcomics is that no two computer monitors will display color the same way, and what looks clear and separate on your monitor might not separate on the monitors of your audience.

WC20: Tell me about the software and tablets you use. Are the tools important?

IS: I use Photoshop, which is pretty much the industry standard, and a Wacom tablet and stylus. While it is possible to color with a mouse, it is needlessly difficult. A small tablet will run you about $100 and is much, much more useful than even a high-end mouse for coloring. Really, there is no comparison.

WC20: Coloring a webcomic is usually done in RGB rather than CMYK. What's the difference, and how does it affect your coloring?

IS: Well, RGB is used for Web-based illustrations due to the larger range of colors you can get than with CMYK. In fact, RGB uses more colors than can be printed, which is why print comics are usually colored in CMYK—with CMYK, you know what the final result will look like.

There is a certain range of colors you can use in RGB that you wouldn't want to use in CMYK, provided that the webcomic was never intended for print—basically, colors so dark that they would put too much ink on a printed page and would risk running and smearing.

If the goal is indeed to eventually have the webcomic in print, then it is probably best to simply paint in CMYK, creating a separate RGB file afterward for the webcomic page that will be put up on the Web. There is much less of a change of colors converting from CMYK to RGB than from RGB to CMYK.

WC20: When converting from webcomic color to print color, is there more to it than just changing the color space?

IS: The biggest thing you will notice quite often when converting RGB files to CMYK is that the colors will seem more muted and muddy. This is due to the fact that many of the colors that you can use in RGB will convert to their nearest print equivalent in CMYK. This is another good reason to be Spartan in your use of muddy and muted tones, if you are thinking ahead to a print collection.

Brighter, lighter colors won't change too much from RGB to CMYK as compared to the darker colors.

Lettering

Finally, speech balloons, lettering, sound effects, and captions are applied (Figure 9.5). See the following sidebar for a guest article from professional letterer Johnny Lowe and learn how pro lettering can make all the difference.

Electronic Lettering

Guest-written by Johnny Lowe

Since we're talking about comics on the computer, it's only natural we talk about lettering on the computer as well. Most letterers swear by Adobe Illustrator, though there's also CorelDraw, Inkscape, and Manga Studio; some even use Photoshop. It depends on what you're familiar with—and of course, your budget.

Fonts

What about fonts? Well, you want to utilize fonts specifically designed for comics—fonts with a "hand-lettered" look. Yes, most comics today are lettered on the computer, but they don't look "typeset," like the text

Figure 9.5 The final lettered page in all its glory.

in this paragraph (Figure 9.6). These fonts are designed for comic books and generally are all caps (though many cool upper/lowercase fonts are available), and many include alternate characters.

For instance, say you want to type the word "commander" (Figure 9.7). As you type out the letters of the word, type the first "m." Then, while simultaneously pressing the Shift key, type the second "m." Look close and you'll see the second "m" is just slightly different from the first. It's subtle, but it contributes to the hand-lettered look.

Comicbookfonts.com (Comicraft) and Blambot.com are two excellent sites for comics fonts. Many Blambot fonts are free, but Comicraft frequently features special offers on its selections. And both sites include numerous how-to tips on most any lettering question that might turn up.

One last thing—despite the fact the name of the font includes the word "Comic," never, ever even consider Comic Sans for lettering your comic book—or even someone else's comic. Because if you do—bad, very bad things will happen to you and your dog.

The Basics

No matter what software you choose for lettering, there are certain basics. First, decide what font is most appropriate for your comic— sometimes different styles are used for different characters (remember Walt Kelly's comic strip *Pogo*?). Don't go crazy with every character speaking with a different "look," however. As with most things—moderation.

Decide on the size and leading (vertical space between lines) for your fonts. While a font at 6.25 pt. size and 7.5 pt. leading works for print, you might want to up the size a few points for best viewing on the computer screen—try several examples at different sizes/leading and see what works best for the font you've chosen.

Dialogue requires text, word balloons, and their corresponding tails, so you'll make a text box, type in the dialogue, center it, and then "stack" it so the text is roughly a diamond shape (with the middle lines wider than the top and bottom). But don't have too much text in a single balloon; break it up into two or perhaps three balloons. This can also be done for pacing, to give the speech a pause, or "beat," between sentences.

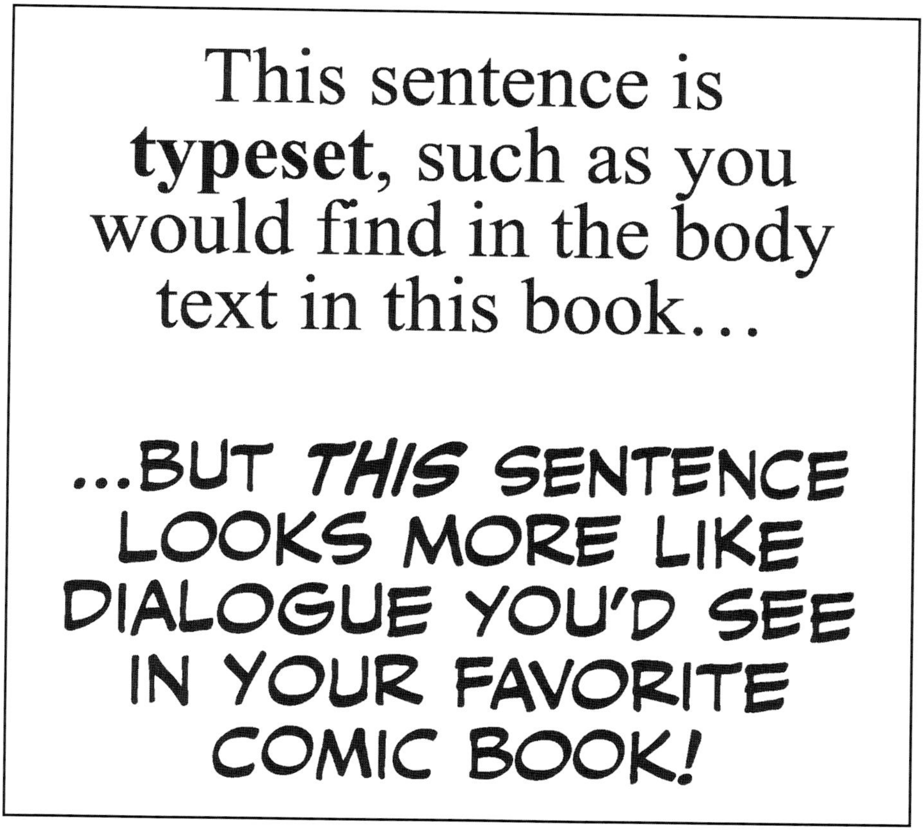

Figure 9.6

A contrast between typeset lettering and webcomics lettering.

This sentence is **typeset**, such as you would find in the body text in this book...

...BUT *THIS* SENTENCE LOOKS MORE LIKE DIALOGUE YOU'D SEE IN YOUR FAVORITE COMIC BOOK!

Figure 9.7

An example of alternate characters contributing to that hand-lettered look.

LOOK *CLOSELY* AT BOTH "M'S" IN "COMMANDER" IN THIS WORD BALLOON!

NOTE THAT THE SECOND "M" IS *SLIGHTLY* DIFFERENT.

Once you've typed the dialogue for the balloon, go back and utilize alternate characters as mentioned above on every other instance of a specific letter—again, for the hand-lettered feel. One thing to remember with the uppercase "I" (which you'll get generally by typing Shift and "I" together, but it depends on the font)—use the version with the "crossbars" (the horizontal bars at the top and bottom of the letter) only with the word "I" or a contraction such as "I'll" or "I've." All other instances will be the plain old "I" that more or less looks like a lowercase "L." Of course you don't have to do this, but it's a style thing most letterers abide by.

Create your balloons, make tails to join them to that point close to the mouth of the person speaking, and then you're getting somewhere. If your artist is on the ball, he will have placed the characters in the panel so that the first person speaking is on the left, the second person speaking to the right, etc. Sometimes, however, they do not do this (or leave a decent amount of space for the lettering), and you will have to juggle things to fit—while at the same time not covering pertinent areas of the art.

If you use sound effects (SFX) in your comic, again, the choice of font is important. If you have an explosion of some sort, you want a big, bad, bold font (e.g., Biff Bam Boom or BadaboomBB) that will communicate the sound and feel of the blast—and not something like Times Bold, which only shows you really didn't put much thought into it.

The Results

The best lettering is lettering that doesn't get noticed; that is, the fonts complement the story, the balloons don't cover up important parts of the art (don't put word balloons over girls!), and balloon placement always furthers the readability of the story. Whether it's on paper or online, lettering is an important part of a comic—there is an art to it, after all.

The Webcomics 2.0 Interview: *Girl Genius*

Girl Genius (www.girlgeniusonline.com), a "Gaslamp Fantasy" comic book, jumped from the independent comic scene to the Web in 2005. Instantly, creators Phil and Kaja Foglio became the poster children for the print-to-Web transition. Today, *Girl Genius* is an extraordinarily popular webcomic that supports multiple graphic novel collections.

The interviewees are Phil and Kaja Foglio, creators of *Girl Genius*.

Webcomics 2.0: *Girl Genius* made the leap from print to the Web and has become extraordinarily popular. To what do you attribute its success?

Phil & Kaja Foglio: Let's start with the fact that *Girl Genius* was already doing pretty well as a periodical, selling six to eight thousand copies per issue. We had three collections in print by 2005, with a dramatic spike in collection sales every time a new comic was published.

While sales of the individual issues were good, most of the profit from the line came from the trade collections. It had gotten to the point where the quarterly periodicals were more like a self-supporting ad for the trades. By dropping the periodical and posting the comic online, we're able to reach a larger audience with new content three days a week instead of four times a year.

WC20: What has been the reaction, if any, from traditional comic book shops?

PKF: At the time—mixed. Some shops were very disappointed and saw the move as a lack of faith in their businesses as a method of reaching customers. However, others were quite supportive, reporting that their collection sales had been steadily growing, while their periodical sales of our titles were leveling off. And then of course there are always a number of shops that don't carry much of the independent titles anyway, and they hardly noticed.

Now that a couple of years have passed, and the collections continue to sell steadily, we hear a lot about how keeping everything in print and available has helped the shops develop new steady customers.

WC20: And now the webcomic is in turn supporting new print collections. How can this be, if readers can still read for free online?

PKF: Reading online is fun, and free, once you've covered the "needs a computer and the Internet" part, but there's something uniquely satisfying about holding a book in your hand. Higher-resolution graphics, control over pacing, and not needing to sit in an office chair are only a few of the bonuses.

The other aspect of being online is numbers. Even if only 10% of your readers choose to buy a book, when your total readership is orders of magnitude larger than it was, it still translates into increased sales.

WC20: How can a struggling print comic creator know that the Web is the right move for them?

PKF: If they're struggling, then the Web is likely to be just what they need. The costs of providing content on a website are so much less than the printing and distribution required for periodicals, and with no shelf-life worries.

WC20: What other projects are both of you working on?

PKF: We're getting more of our older work back into print. *Myth Adventures*, the comic adaptation of Robert Asprin's novel *Another Fine Myth*, was published by WaRP Graphics and Donning in the '80s. We will be bringing it out in October as one single giant color collection.

In March 2008 we have the reprint of *Buck Godot: PSmIth* in color, as well as a black and white collection of the eight issues of *Buck Godot: Gallimaufry*.

There are also plans underway to do some more work with the Girl Genius Radio Plays, but that's not finalized enough to be worth talking about yet.

Saving the Art

When doing art, whether scanning it in or doing it entirely on computer, save the raw file as you go in the graphics program's native format: in other words, PSD for Photoshop and MSD for Manga Studio. Then, when you're completely done with the webcomics installment, you need to save in two formats. First, save in TIF at 400 dpi and the original page dimensions. This file is important for T-shirts, the collected book edition, and other ancillary products.

Then, save under a different filename as a 100 dpi JPG. This is going to be suitable for the Web, so the page dimensions depend on what size you want on the screen. Letterbox or 4:3 format is 640 × 480. A standard comic book page, horizontally visible on most computers but requiring a bit of scrolling downward to read it all, is 1500 × 2200. A comic strip format all depends on how large your panels are. An infinite canvas webcomic can be just about any size you want it to be.

Experiment with different dimensions under different filenames (making sure Constrain Proportions is checked) and figure out what's going to look good for your readers. Once you decide on dimensions, stick with it unless your webcomic changes format.

The Bleed

When preparing digital files for print collections, there's an important concept to keep in mind, and no, it's not painful. The *bleed* is the extra art around the border of a comic that is lost when the printing machines make the book. During the page-cutting process, you'll lose a certain amount of art around the edges. There are two solutions to the bleed issue.

The first is to continue to draw all the way to the edge of the paper, but make sure that no important details appear on the edges and no speech balloons or captions would be cut off. This is called *full bleed art*. The other solution is to inset the artwork in the center of the page and put a thick border around it, .125 inches from the edge. The cutting will all happen outside of this border, so you don't lose any art. This is called *bordered art*.

Single-panel or strip-format webcomics are almost always bordered; manga and Western-style full-page art is sometimes full-bleed, sometimes not. It all depends on the style of the particular webcomic.

Infinite Canvas to Finite Book Page

Translating an infinite canvas webcomic (one that can travel in any direction on the computer screen and can have any size panels) is a challenge. Print, obviously, is not infinite, so some compromises may have to be made. You may need to fit multiple installments on a single page. You may elect to print your book in a different size, such as horizontally (as many newspaper comics are reprinted). You may have to chop up a single installment across multiple book pages. Or you may conclude that print is just not the best venue for your eclectic work, and you will have to live without.

Miscellaneous Art

Other than the art in the webcomic itself, there are several other elements on your webcomic site where your art skills will come in handy.

Art Extras

You've done character sketches, attempts at a specific pose, or even an entire installment that just didn't get the effect you were looking for. Don't let these art extras go to waste—put them on the site, for the fans! Many webcomics collectives have specific sections on your webcomic's page for sketches and other extras. By allowing your readers a glimpse into the creative process, you let them feel like active participants. Also, giving readers this kind of insight just may be the last step toward another webcomics creator being born!

Character Profiles

Many webcomics collectives offer a section to show off your characters. These character sections can include original pinups or head shots of the cast members and a short description of their personalities. Feel free to adapt the character bible the writer put together when creating your webcomic (see Chapter 8, in the section "The Character Bible"). Consider including links to key webcomics that showcase these characters.

When writing the descriptions, just be sure to leave out any spoilery information revealed in the character bible but not yet revealed in the webcomic itself. It never hurts to consult with the writer about what you can and can't say. Even better, let the writer write the thing, and you can make it look nice for the site. If you're a one-man army, then you'll have to talk things over with yourself. Just be sure nobody's around.

Do the Evolution

As you get into the habit of drawing your webcomic regularly, you'll find your art evolving and changing, sometimes consciously, sometimes unconsciously. Don't worry about fighting these changes, and don't worry about forcing yourself to emulate your old style. This is you getting better, faster, and more sure of yourself. Whether the current installments match the archives is irrelevant. The evolution of your art will ultimately make the webcomic better. Besides, you'll know you've really arrived when fans start complaining that "your old stuff was better."

Here's how Sam Romero's art evolved from the very beginning of *Edge the Devilhunter's* run on Graphic Smash (Figure 9.8) to the original short story for this book (Figure 9.9).

Figure 9.8 Here's how *Edge the Devilhunter* looked in its original incarnation on Graphic Smash.

Figure 9.9 And here's how Romero reworked the design for this book in his modern style.

Conclusion

As we said in Chapter 8, people come to webcomics for the art. Though art skill isn't as important to a webcomic's success as a print comic, it is important to be clean and consistent in whatever presentation you choose. Practice and repetition are important for developing skills and taking your art where you want to be. Ultimately, expressing yourself through webcomics art will fulfill you in a way that art for a corporation can't possibly—because it's your art and you own it.

10

Getting Published

OK, you have a creation ready to reveal to the world. Where do you put it? That's a complicated question. There are three avenues for your webcomic, and each carries with it numerous advantages and disadvantages.

First, let's define our terms. *Webcomics hosting service* refers to a free (usually with additional fee-based features available) website that anyone can sign up for and is designed to publish webcomics easily. A *webcomics collective* is a hosting service that is by invitation only. Collectives invite only a select few comics into their fold each year, but they often provide benefits that an all-inclusive hosting service does not.

Finally, *self-publishing* refers to securing a web host, installing your own comic publishing software, and doing everything on your own: a true do-it-yourself enterprise. It's perfectly OK to use a combination of approaches. Publish your webcomic yourself and put it on a hosting service or two at the same time. The more eyeballs that see your work, the better.

What Is FTP?

Regardless of the approach you take, it's almost certain that somewhere along the line you'll be using FTP. FTP stands for *File Transfer Protocol,* and it's a way to move large files from your computer to the server that hosts your webcomic or vice versa. When you sign up for the site that hosts your comic, you'll usually be given FTP information. Once you download and install your FTP program (CoreFTP at www.coreftp.com is a great, free choice), enter that info, save it, connect, and drag and drop your comic pages wherever they tell you the pages go. It's just that simple.

Note that some hosting services and collectives don't let you use FTP. You'll be forced to use their web form to upload pages, and if you have a huge archive, that could be cumbersome. Always ask about an FTP option; there may be an undocumented FTP site that the host will tell you about.

In Figures 10.1 through 10.3 are step-by-step visuals for dragging and dropping files to an FTP site.

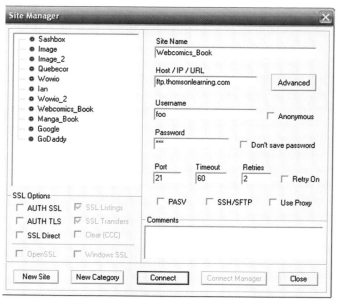

Figure 10.1

Click New Site and enter the FTP address, the login, and password provided by the host.

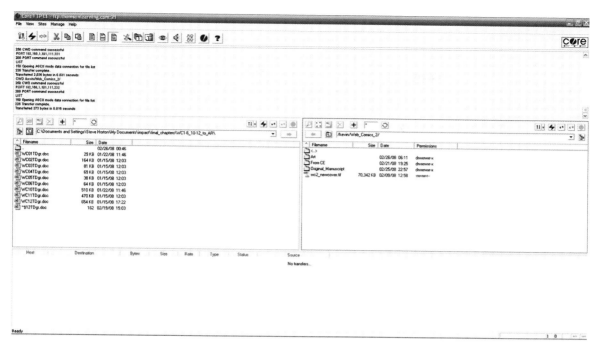

Figure 10.2 Click the lightning bolt that represents Connect. Navigate to the appropriate folder.

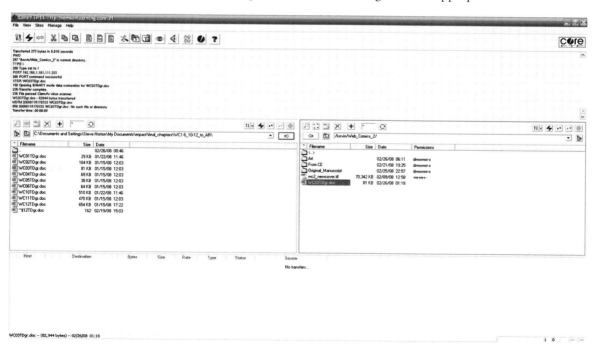

Figure 10.3 Either click on the file and click on the right arrow, or drag and drop files to the right-hand pane. The files are now transferred.

Webcomics Hosting Services

A webcomic hosting service is simply a website that you register on, like any other website, and which then lets you upload and display your webcomics alongside many others. It takes the need for all that technical knowledge out of hosting the comic yourself. This is a great first choice for a webcomics creator because there are no long-term agreements or anything locking you in. You can always decide to go it alone later.

Webcomics Hosting Services: Plusses and Minuses

Here's a table of the five major webcomics hosting services, and their plusses and minuses. Some columns aren't self explanatory. *Revenue Sharing* is the capability for the site to pay the creator in some way; *Multiple Uploads* refers to uploading many pages at once; *Downloadable Archives* means recovering your entire archive of comics easily; Customization is redesigning the page itself based on your standards; and *RSS* (Really Simple Syndication) *Feed* is a way to subscribe to the information in multiple sites at the same time.

	ComicSpace	*ComicGenesis*	*DrunkDuck*	*LiveJournal*
Cost	Free+Premium	Free	Free	Free+Premium
Ease of Setup	Easy	Easy	Easy	Medium
Can run own ads	Premium	No	*	No
Revenue Sharing	Yes	No	No	No
Multiple Uploads	Unlimited	Unlimited	10	Unlimited
Downloadable Archives	Yes	Yes	No	Yes
Customization	Extensive	Extensive	Limited	Moderate
Blog	Yes	No	Yes	Yes
Forum	Yes	Yes	Yes	No
RSS Feed	Yes	Yes	No	Yes

*It's possible to run a banner ad on a DrunkDuck page with a little bit of code in the HTML template. However, such ads are not compatible with the "home page" feature, which includes the blog and message board. The home page must be turned off for ads to work correctly.

Using a hosting service is one of the cheapest methods of webcomic publication, and it also takes the burden out of setup, installation, and programming, giving you time to focus on creation and promotion.

Right now there are three major websites that offer free comics hosting. In addition, many webcomic creators have adopted a blog service, LiveJournal, as a de facto hosting service, so we're including it.

None of these sites take away any intellectual property rights. That means that even though these sites publish your work, you retain ownership. This is important for many reasons, not the least of which is that others cannot exploit your creation for any purpose without your permission.

ComicSpace

Formerly separate websites ComicSpace (created by Josh Roberts) and Webcomics Nation (created by Joey Manley), ComicSpace (www.comicspace.com) is relaunching in the second quarter of 2008 as an all-in-one solution for webcomics creators, social networkers interested in comics, or both. The list of features, costs, and benefits is still in flux at publication time, but here's what we can tell you.

ComicSpace provides free webcomics hosting and integrated social networking (think of a normal webcomic hosting service combined with a MySpace for comics). Creators can make a dedicated forum and blog for their webcomic. There's a ton of automation. There will be additional features that will cost extra, but all of the important functionality will be free. The kicker is that anyone with a ComicSpace site earns an advertising revenue share based on how popular their site is.

Check www.comicspace.com by mid-2008 for details of what this site provides. After the relaunch, this will be the no-brainer choice for all webcomics creators.

ComicGenesis

Previously known as Keenspace, ComicGenesis (www.comicgenesis.com) is the free cousin of Keenspot, the webcomics collective mentioned later in this chapter. Anyone can publish comics on ComicGenesis. There's a lot of customization possible with the look and feel of your ComicGenesis page, and the site provides FTP info for uploading numerous comics at once.

One drawback is that ComicGenesis runs its own ads, so it's impossible to earn revenue from advertising. However, it is OK to promote merchandise, convention appearances, and other revenue-generating objects on your ComicGenesis site.

Several of the highest-quality and most-popular ComicGenesis webcomics have graduated into a coveted spot on Keenspot. If you're looking for an avenue into that exclusive club, then ComicGenesis is one route to get there.

DrunkDuck

Created by Dylan Squires and now owned by Platinum Comics, DrunkDuck (www.drunkduck.com) has an enormous social aspect that makes it a draw. The user-friendly and iconic interface makes it easy to sign up and upload comics. The large DrunkDuck community is always open to new projects. What's interesting about DrunkDuck is that it has a commenting feature below each page of your comic, and it's not difficult to find yourself with 10 or more comments when a new installment goes up.

Getting featured on the front page of DrunkDuck leads to a huge readership spike, and a good webcomic can often ride this spike to permanent popularity. The friendly moderators will also post milestones on the front page, such as when your strip reaches 50 installments.

It is possible to run ads on a DrunkDuck page; however, this is not automated, and you must obtain the code snippet from the ad site and paste it somewhere in your page template. Keep in mind that ads won't work correctly when your home page is turned on. The home page includes the forum and the blog, so you'll have to choose between ads or the social element. Also, most of the page is taken up by Platinum's own advertising, so self-advertising might not be effective.

One big drawback is that you can only upload 10 pages at a time, and only via the site's Web interface. Huge archives will take all day to get on the site.

DrunkDuck often sponsors free group tables at major comic conventions. This is a great value-ad that might make this site worth a try.

LiveJournal

Though LiveJournal is ostensibly a blog community, there are many creators who have chosen to make LiveJournal their webcomics home. The community is built in, it's easy to set up an account and post comics, and purchasing any of the premium features is absolutely not necessary. The nice thing about having webcomics on LiveJournal is that members frequently share each other's comics through links. For instance, one person might post a Supergirl drawing, and that might lead to thousands of users posting their own Supergirl drawings, creating a big link chain; that sort of thing happens there a lot. If you're already into blogging, this is just a natural extension.

The above Supergirl chain is an example of an Internet meme, or Internet-based pop-culture concept that spreads like wildfire. Webcomics have given Internet memes a comic book angle, and LiveJournal is where most of the webcomics brand of memes are found.

The drawback of LiveJournal that it won't let you run ads of any kind, but you can link to your book or convention appearance.

Webcomics Collectives

A webcomics collective is similar to a webcomic hosting service, with one important difference. Collectives are by invitation only. Either you must submit your comic or they find you and invite you based on merit. Some collectives regularly add and subtract webcomics, while others remain static for years.

An advantage of a collective is that there is strength in numbers. It allows a tight-knit group of creators to work together on promotion, convention appearances, advertising, and merchandise.

Unlike hosting services, most collectives are designed to make some sort of revenue for each of its members. There are exceptions: Some collectives simply go for that studio feel, and its creators don't actively seek income except away from the group—for example, with day jobs.

The following sections discuss the major collectives and how to get noticed by them.

Keenspot

Perhaps the granddaddy of comics collectives, Keenspot (www.keenspot.com) is the brainchild of Chris Crosby and Darren Bleuel. (See Crosby's interview both here and in Chapter 2, "Humor.") Many of the Web's most popular webcomics creations began life at Keenspot. Some remain, and some have gone on to greener pastures, but the Keenspot legacy remains.

Keenspot has also ventured into graphic novel publishing, merchandising, and web animation. The latter is in tandem with Comflix, a Web-based comic book animation site. Also, a completely separate set of animations can be found in cell phone form on Verizon's V-CAST network.

To get on Keenspot, you usually must have been published successfully elsewhere. The site looks for quality as well as popularity. Creators share in the site's revenue and get to take advantage of all of the site's promotional opportunities.

The Webcomics 2.0 Interview: Keenspot

Chris Crosby is the co-CEO of Keenspot.

WC20: There are more webcomics collectives and webcomics in general every day. What is Keenspot doing to stay fresh and new and compete amidst all these contenders?

Chris Crosby: Truthfully, not much. Keenspot does dabble in new things, but in general it finds what seems to work and sticks with it for the long haul. Keenspot is virtually the same as it was six years ago; [*it*] doesn't feel the need to constantly shake things up in order to compete with other webcomics. If "slow and steady wins the race" is right, Keenspot will win the webcomics race handily. And if not, it will die a horrific death in a tar pit someday.

WC20: How often does a new comic get signed on to Keenspot?

CC: Three to five per year on average. Just a little bit more than the average newspaper collective.

WC20: What are you all looking for these days?

CC: As always, Keenspot is looking for consistency, wide appeal, and whatever we happen to consider "high quality." If the comic has a large existing readership, that doesn't hurt.

WC20: Do you feel that a webcomic must eventually strike out away from a collective and on its own, or do collectives remain important as popularity increases?

CC: No; neither. Unless your collective is unusually limiting in what you can do, there's no reason you can't be incredibly successful as part of that collective. Likewise, I don't see being part of a collective as terribly important to the success of a webcomic. Certain collectives can provide a big boost to your comic's popularity and can help you in other areas, but you can do virtually the same or better on your own if you're willing to put in the time and effort.

WC20: What other projects is Keenspot working on as a company, other than ComicGenesis?

CC: Keenspot's main non-comics project at the moment is a major animation production initiative in our Keentoons division. We're producing 100+ short animated episodes for distribution on mobile phones in association with mobile video distributor ThunderSquid. We launched with about 50 Keentoons mobisodes in August, and those can currently be seen on Verizon V-CAST in the U.S. and on O2 Mobile in the UK, among many other carriers. They've been very successful so far, based on the earliest reports we've received, and we're very excited about this new platform.

We're also continuing to make some headway into Hollywood, slowly but surely.

Blank Label Comics

Casual observers might call Blank Label Comics (www.blanklabelcomics.com) a spinoff of Keenspot. After all, every member has been a part of Keenspot in the past, and a few of them left Keenspot specifically to form Blank Label. It's not really a spinoff, though. Blank Label is designed to do things the right way, from advertising to promotion to revenue generation.

One 2008 Blank Label development is that the newest entry for each of its comics is now visible on the front page; no longer are you required to visit each creator's page individually. You're going to want to, though, because that's where you'll read the archives.

Blank Label features David Willis of *Shortpacked!* and Howard Tayler of *Schlock Mercenary* (both interviewed in Chapter 3, "Humor"), Greg Dean's *Real Life Comics*, Paul Southworth's *Ugly Hill*, Steve Troop's *Melonpool*, and Paul Taylor's *Wapsi Square*.

Getting into Blank Label is difficult; only a couple of members have been added since its inception. Having lost two creators to Scott Kurtz's Halfpixel collective, though, Blank Label may be looking for new blood at some point.

Modern Tales

The Modern Tales family of sites includes Modern Tales (www.modern-tales.com), Graphic Smash (www.graphicsmash.com), Serializer (www.serial-izer.net), and Girlamatic (www.girlamatic.com). Modern Tales is owned by Joey Manley and therefore is also part of the relaunched ComicSpace. As of press time, it's unclear exactly how the Modern Tales collectives will be integrated with ComicSpace. It appears that each site will remain by invitation only, and it's likely there will still be advantages to being a part of Modern Tales, rather than an independent ComicSpace webcomic.

Each site is geared toward a different genre. Modern Tales is the all-purpose site. Graphic Smash is action-adventure webcomics. Serializer is "art" comics, and Girlamatic is for women-focused comics (though the creators need not be women).

Applying to be on a Modern Tales family site is as simple as contacting each individual editor. Editor e-mails can be located on the blogs of each site.

ACT-I-VATE

Launched in early 2006 by veteran comics creators Dean Haspiel, Michel Fiffe, and six other creators, ACT-I-VATE (http://community.livejournal.com/act_i_vate/) is a LiveJournal-based webcomics community. The webcomics you'll find here are generally for mature audiences only, but that's not always the case. The one thing they truly have in common is quality. Everything on ACT-I-VATE is astoundingly good.

ACT-I-VATE even had its own section of the "Infinite Canvas: The Art of Webcomics" exhibit. See Chapter 13, "Just Create," for more on this art show, which ran from September 14, 2007, to January 24, 2008.

One of the requirements for being a part of ACT-I-VATE is that you have to create the entire webcomic yourself. Also, because it's by invitation only, it's a good idea to become a part of the LiveJournal webcomics community if you aren't already. Get noticed with a quality LiveJournal webcomic, and the ACT-I-VATE people will find you. There are 23 members as of press time, and more come and go all the time.

The work that ACT-I-VATE has done has even inspired the formation of new webcomics collectives. Though it came along much later than other groups, those associated with ACT-I-VATE seem to be latter-day pioneers.

The Chemistry Set

Conceived as a response to ACT-I-VATE by Vito Delsante and his friends, The Chemistry Set inches toward the traditional by being writer focused and allowing writer–artist teams. That's the only thing mainstream about this group, though, as its eclectic mix rivals any other.

The Chemistry Set is also notable for veering into print comics after *The Surreal Adventures of Edgar Allen Poo* became a print comic through Image/Shadowline.

This group is always on the lookout for more talent. See the following sidebar for an interview with four of the creators behind The Chemistry Set.

The Webcomics 2.0 Interview: The Chemistry Set

The Chemistry Set (www.chemsetcomics.com) is a writer-focused webcomics collective consisting of writer-artist teams on each webcomic. We managed to land four ChemSet members for this mammoth interview: Steven Goldman, Vito Delsante, Dwight MacPherson, and Chris Arrant.

Webcomics 2.0: How did The Chemistry Set come about?

Vito Delsante: As a reaction to ACT-I-VATE. The initial group that started out are all friends of mine, and I was looking to do an online strip with one of them, but it was by invite only and all cartoonists that were writing their own stories. I went home, sent an e-mail to Chris Arrant, and said, "What is preventing us from doing a writer-based comics collective?" Before I even got a reply (which was fairly quick), I had e-mailed Neil [*Kleid*] with a simple tease, "Are you interested in doing an online comic?" or something similarly vague. After that, the three of us threw ideas around, names of contemporaries, and we went about seeing who was available. Out of all of the folks we asked, only one couldn't commit to something at that moment, but I think he'll be with us soon.

Chris Arrant: I can't lie—I blame Dean [*Haspiel*], Dan [*Goldman*], and the ACT-I-VATE crew. The idea of doing a webcomic had been in my mind as a possibility for some time, but seeing ACT-I-VATE blossom so powerfully made a "possible" a "tangible" thing worth reaching for. At the time, ACT-I-VATE was an auteurs-only kind of thing so the idea of a counterpoint—a site with a writer and artist team—seemed an ideal match.

W20: *Surreal Adventures of Edgar Allan Poo* landed a publishing deal and came out as a comic book. This is an important distinction from self-publishing strip archives. How did the deal at Image/Shadowline happen?

Dwight MacPherson: Earlier this year, I pitched *Edgar Allan Poo* to Jim Valentino and Kris Simon at Shadowline. They fell in love with the book and signed us almost immediately. Volume 1 sold extremely well, and the second volume is currently in production. Good times.

W20: How do you find new talent for The Chemistry Set?

Steven Goldman: I've only brought one new name to the ChemSet so far—Stacey Garratt—but I'm always keeping my eye out for people with a unique voice and who have a real story to tell. I know ACT-I-VATE's Nikki Cook from my Brooklyn days, and she and Stacey have been cooking up a magnum opus for some time called *The Wings of Juano Diaz*. Nikki's been feeding me teases for a while, and just those glimpses were enough to make me want to tempt Stacey into joining. She teaches writing to teens in Minneapolis and brings heartbreaking poetry to her work. She's up there with the likes of Nate Powell, [who wrote] *Tiny Giants*, Gilbert Hernandez, [who wrote] *Palomar*, and Jason Lutes, [who wrote] *Berlin*. That said, I want to see things in comics I haven't seen before, and I want to bring creators who can work that magic to the site.

VD: It's really a matter, for me, of two things. One, do they have a presence online or are they working toward bringing something to the online community, and two, and possibly more important, do I respect the previous work of the creator? Do I enjoy it? At the end of the day, I feel like my name is somewhere on the page, and I don't want to be ashamed of or apologize for something we put up there. I know we all feel the same way because we can all be very, very picky about what we want to submit to the other members. In the case of Dwight and *Surreal Adventures of Edgar Allan Poo*, I was initially put off by the name, but the actual strips (the few I read at the time) really entertained me, so I was willing to try to talk the others into it. Luckily enough, there was no arm twisting needed.

CA: I scour the Internet a lot, for fun and for my comics journalism work [*Arrant writes about comics for Publishers Weekly and Newsarama.com*], and in that I find numerous talents that I end up following. Some of those I end up covering in my journalism endeavors, some I want to work with on comics myself, and now a third category exists of people I want to work with in The Chemistry Set collective. Of our current lineup, I proudly claim Andrew Drilon's *Kare-Kare Komiks* as someone I found and brought into the fold to great result.

WC20: Several of The Chemistry Set comics experiment with webcanvas. For example, *1 Way Ticket* is all ticket-shaped panels (for the most part). Why the break from a traditional panel layout, and does this interfere with print collection plans?

SG: Dean Haspiel and Michel Fiffe have already proved that you can rock an experimental design with their comics *Immortal* and *Panorama* and then bring them into a standard paper format afterward, as they've done with Image's *Brawl*. To paraphrase Kubrick, you have to learn to stop worrying and love the medium for what it is: giving each page a dovetail or hook, since your readers see them one at a time [*and*] learning to drip tension down the window with every vertical panel. A blank browser window is full of possibilities, so why not write the story for its strengths and worry later about how it'll all work in print?

For the record, knowing Dan Warner's design savvy, I suspect *1 Way Ticket* will make a sharp book when it's done.

VD: I'm not sure how it affects future print plans, but the Web, specifically the webpage, is an open canvas to play with format. And lately, publishers like AdHouse Books and Picturebox are pushing what you can do in print, so I think that if we're lucky enough to get any of The Chemistry Set strips collected and published, layout won't pose a problem.

CA: As writer for *1 Way Ticket*, I can say that the ticket-shaped panels that we segued to around page 20 was an attempt by myself and artist Dan Warner to try different layouts than the standard print page size. If you notice, though, they are of such size that when a print edition is made, then the four ticket-shaped panels can be joined to form a standard full page.

WC20: What other projects are some of the Chemistry Set creators working on?

SG: Part of the reason that I've been so quiet on the comics front is that I've been developing a few graphic novel projects at once, including long- and short-form stories for my series *Styx Taxi*, a corporate thriller, a magical realist fable for children, and a prose novel that'll unravel slowly online.

VD: I'm actually trying to break in new talent with my next two strips. Both artists have never had anything in print, and I think that will change after their strips go live. The first new strip, *FCHS*, is based loosely on my life in a small town in Pennsylvania and my high school life. Rachel Freire is doing the art, and we have some previews of her art, a mix between Jaime Hernandez, Dan DeCarlo, and Alex Toth, on the site already. That will be starting in December [*2007*]. In January/February [*2008*], Edi Torres will join me for an adventure strip called *The Doberman*, which takes place in Nazi Germany during the last days of WW2. Like *The Gloom* by Tony Lee and Dan Boultwood, this will be one of our first forays into the superhero comic genre.

CA: I've fallen in love with short storytelling in comics and recently had a story in *24SEVEN*, Volume 2 from Image, and I have stories in three upcoming anthologies that I'm equally excited about. Besides that, I have some longer stories in the works, but they're still in the process.

Self-Publishing

It's difficult to go it alone, on your own website. This is, however, the route that many of the biggest webcomics today have taken. By not becoming lost in a sea of similar comics on the same website, someone self-publishing can stand out. Also, those control freaks among you will find that self-publishing offers the highest degree of customization. The sky is the limit for how you want to design your site and publish your comic.

Self-publishing means that you share revenue only with your team and nobody else. You make all the decisions every step of the way. You control all advertising, page design, layout, editorial content, and so on. However, self-publishers can fall victim to being lost in the sea of the Internet at large. Standing out through marketing and promotion becomes even more critical. If this seems daunting, especially for a first-timer, you might want to consider a hosting service or collective. For those that can handle it, though, this is an excellent choice.

Choosing a Web Host

You can design your site on your own machine, so it's not necessary to have a web host beforehand, but at some point during the process you'll have to choose one. A *web host* is a company that hosts your website in a remote location, usually in a building of computers called a *server farm*. Often, but not always, your web host is where you'll purchase the domain name you'll be using (such as www.thedriftercomic.com). Web hosts charge a monthly or yearly fee for hosting and usually a yearly fee for the domain name. Expect to pay around six bucks a month for the former and 10 bucks a year for the latter.

Make sure when choosing a web host that you don't pick one that puts ad banners anywhere on your site that you can't get rid of. These banners will mess with your site design, and ultimately the cost savings just isn't worth it. Why pay $3 for a site full of ads when you could pay $6 for one without?

One recommendation for a web host is GoDaddy (www.godaddy.com). You might have seen the Super Bowl ads. They're inexpensive and provide numerous payment options. Don't go for the expensive add-ons, except for the domain name, of course.

Once you've got a web host and domain name ready to go, the next step is designing your site.

Hard Coding

If you're at all familiar with modern Web design, you'll find that setting up a website using cascading style sheets (CSS) is not that difficult, especially since you're doing it for yourself and not a picky corporate client. If you don't know anything at all about Web design, though, all is not lost. There is one application you can install easily on your website that will give you many of the same features that a comics hosting service or collective provides and all of the control. It's called ComicPress.

ComicPress

A creation of webcomic creator Tyler Martin, ComicPress (www.mind-faucet.com/comicpress) is a theme of the popular blog software WordPress. WordPress prides itself on being super-easy to install, and ComicPress is equally easy to install after WordPress is there. Both require just a tiny bit of knowledge about database software MySQL.

Setting It Up

First you go into your web host's control panel and create a database in MySQL. Give it a name, create a username and password, tell the WordPress installation what they are, and you're set. One additional wrinkle when using GoDaddy: When setting up a database, you can't put in localhost for the host as you can most other places. Instead, GoDaddy will provide you with one in the form of mysql???.secureserver.net, where ??? is a number.

Then you install ComicPress in the Templates folder and choose that template in your WordPress administration. Put all your comics in the comic folder with the correct date format that ComicPress provides, and you're set.

ComicPress Limitations

One limitation of ComicPress is that it can handle only one comic per day out of the box, so sites with more than one distinct comic are going to run into problems. If another comic is uploaded with the same date, both get put into the same post. Many people have provided hacks or coding additions to ComicPress to fix this and customize it further; check out the ComicPress forum at http://lunchboxfunnies.com/forum/viewforum.php?f=7 for more information.

Uh...I Don't Get It

Again, if all of this is Greek to you, consider one of the other choices for your first webcomic. After you get used to being part of a hosting service or collective, you can always strike out on your own later.

A Final Note on Publishing

Whatever avenue you choose in which to publish your webcomic, don't take half measures. Go all out and devote as much effort as you can to it. If you find yourself hitting a ceiling with the publication environment of your choice, break away and try a different one. Similarly, if you find out that fits like a glove, wear it with pride!

11

Promotion

You've created and launched your webcomics creation. Now comes the part that nobody really loves to do, but everyone needs to do: Promotion! "If you build it, they will come" is the least true axiom in the history of webcomics. You need to put at least as much work into promoting your comic as you do creating it. Let me repeat that for emphasis. Your promotional effort has to be equal to your creative effort.

"But all I want to do is create!" you say. Unfortunately, though creation is the ultimate reason your comic exists, it's not enough. Fortunately, with a little practice, good, nonintrusive promotion is not only possible, but it's relatively painless.

We'll start with the promotion that you can do for free, and then we'll move on to promotion that will cost you a little money up front. Rigging this cost correctly, however, should eventually net you a return greater than the expense.

One final note before we dive in: Merchandising is arguably a form of promotion. For the purposes of this discussion, we've treated merchandising as a separate issue, covered in the next chapter.

No-Cost Promotion

Webcomics, since they reside on the Internet, have a whole host of free promotional tools available. There are many different free ways to show off and extol the virtues of your creation.

A Community of Potential Fans

Community-based promotion is as simple as going to different venues on the Net, such as forums and social networking sites, and talking about your comic in a non-spam way.

Forums

Spread the word about your webcomic! You already post in various forums, right? Put your webcomic in your signature file. If there's a spot in your favorite forum for plugs or self-promotion, put a post there. Please remember not to spam about your comic in places where it is not wanted. This is called *forum whoring* and is frowned upon. Instead, find a topic that interests you and join the discussion in progress. Make friends. People will find out about what you do eventually.

If you don't already post in forums, consider forums where comics creators already hang out and are open to new people. DigitalWebbing (www. digitalwebbing.com), and Panel and Pixel (www.panelandpixel.com) are two examples.

MySpace

MySpace (www.myspace.com), being one of the most popular social networking sites, is a terrific place to promote your comics. Just about anyone and everyone associated with comics has a page here, and many of them check it regularly. It's a great way to get to know people in webcomics, as the right place and the right time can mean your little webcomic can move on up to a print collection from a major publisher, for example.

It should be noted that MySpace has really ramped up its focus on comic books. www.myspace.com/comics/ is a popular starting point and is worth adding to your Friends list straightaway. Keep in mind that this focus is more on corporate print comics, as MySpace has a relationship with Virgin Comics and Dark Horse Comics, among others. However, that doesn't mean you can't use MySpace's comics portal and MySpace in general to promote your webcomic.

Do a Web search for a good MySpace template that fits the mood and theme of your webcomic but isn't too obtrusive. Make sure the art of the webcomic takes center stage, because it's the art that will draw people into the story.

If you want to maintain a running blog associated with your webcomic, MySpace is one place to do that. However, it's not the greatest blog interface in the world. If you're really into blogging, consider one of the dedicated blog sites, and see the section on blogging later in this chapter.

Figure 11.1 is the MySpace page for Smashout Comics, the publishing company owned by the writer of this book.

Figure 11.1
The MySpace home of Steve Horton's Smashout Comics.

ComicSpace

Ahh, now this is more like it. ComicSpace (www.comicspace.com), the all-in-one webcomics site, has a community feature that is similar to but more focused than MySpace. ComicSpace has a ton of webcomics creators onboard. Free of some of the bugs and clutter of MySpace and featuring tools specific to comics, ComicSpace will allow you to post your webcomic for free, promote it in bulletins, and sell original art. A good ComicSpace page for your webcomic will allow it to become more popular, because word of mouth will spread between the people on your Friends list and the Friends lists of others.

ComicSpace allows you to tooncast your webcomic from ComicSpace to other places, such as blogs. What is a tooncast? Briefly, you copy a line of code that ComicSpace provides, and you paste it into a blog post, similar to how sharing a YouTube video on your blog works. This is a quick and easy way to show off your webcomic in multiple venues without having to upload your pages each time. Plus, clicking on the comic in the blog will link back to your ComicSpace page.

ComicSpace is also a good place to post pencil sketches, deleted scenes, character designs, and other art-related tidbits.

As mentioned in Chapter 10, "Getting Published," ComicSpace is relaunching in Q2 2008 with a raft of all-new features. Check the site for all that's new with this resource.

Blogging

A blog, short for weblog, is a site where you post diary-like entries about any subject. The best webcomics blogs offer running commentary from the creators, either about the comic itself or about life in general, sometimes both. While many webcomics collectives and syndicates have blogging built in, some don't. There is a solution: LiveJournal's paid membership (starting at $5/month) allows you to cast the blog on another site, such as your webcomic's location. The drawback to this is that blog comments aren't visible on the comic page itself—you must click through to LiveJournal to see them.

Blogging, in concert with the webcomic itself, is a way to connect to the audience and help them feel closer to you. You're not a faceless corporation; you're a human being with a small business, and a blog is a way to show that you care. Plus, it allows you to comment on what's going on in the world in a way that you might not be able to get across in your webcomic.

Those creating their comic's website themselves or using ComicPress will be able to integrate their blog with their comic more easily. Find out more about creating a website and using ComicPress in Chapter 10, "Getting Published."

There's at least one comic collective that has smashed together the concept of the blog and the webcomic. It's called ACT-I-VATE (Figure 11.2), and it's on LiveJournal. See the "Webcomics Syndicates" section in Chapter 10 for more information on this talented group of people.

Figure 11.2
The ACT-I-VATE collective on LiveJournal showcases eclectic webcomics.

Comments

Sites such as DrunkDuck allow commenting, a feature built into each page of your webcomic. Registered users can voice their feelings about the comic directly. You as a creator can also post comments of your own every day, either as a response to an existing comment or as a commentary of your own. This direct, right-on-the-page conversation goes a long way toward building a community of fans who stop by your webcomic not just to read the latest comic but also to read and participate in the commentary. Figure 11.3 has an example of the comments feature in action.

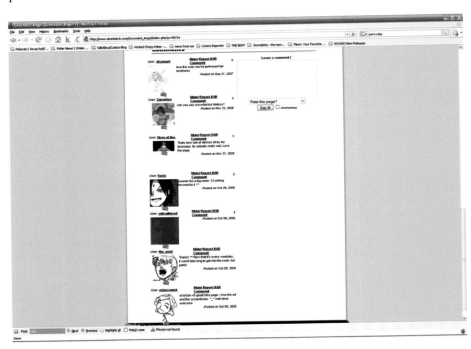

Figure 11.3

Multiple DrunkDuck fans comment on an installment of *Grounded Angel*.

The Power of the Press

Another no-cost promotional tool can have its ups and downs, depending on how things go. Send your webcomics press releases to the various comic media. Submit your comics for review at any number of webcomics review websites. Try to get interviewed by the comics sites that cover webcomics. There's a lot you can do in order to get your webcomic out there and get some face time with the fans. Anything to get them to check you out and get hooked.

Press Releases

Almost all of the comics-related websites run press releases, usually along the side so as to differentiate them from news stories. What's a press release? It's a formal letter announcing some cool aspect of your webcomic, such as the launch, an anniversary, a popularity milestone, a major storyline development, or a reader contest. Press releases should be no more than one page using a 12-point font.

Send the press release as a mass e-mail (using the BCC feature of your e-mail program) to all the comics contacts you can think of. Include the press release as plain text in the body of the e-mail, but also attach the press release in Word format. Also, include a couple of images from the comic as attachments.

It's a good idea to post the press release on your website or social networking site, as well. The Bulletins or Blog feature of MySpace is a good place for it, especially now that your friends can see what you've updated.

See the example press release elsewhere on this page. Here's a rundown of elements you'll need to include in yours.

- The first line of the press release should be a headline, describing your press release. Punch it up as much as possible. You want the headline to be attention grabbing so people read the rest of it. The subject line of the e-mail you send the press release in should be this same headline.

- Continue with the date that the press release will go live, usually the next business day after the day you write it. The following line, For Immediate Release, says that you're OK with the press release going out as soon as the recipient gets it.

- After that, include contact information. One or two people, usually co-creators, go here. Put their real names and e-mails. Don't include phone numbers or home addresses.

- Then comes the body of the press release. Talk about your comic and where to find it. Include quotes from yourself and the other co-creators. Don't go overboard here; get to the point and tell readers why they should check out your webcomic and what makes it interesting.

- Finally, include an About section. Either put in information about your publishing company, if you have one, or put in a short bio for yourself and your co-creator(s). Include a weblink to your company's or your personal website or social networking page.

That's it! Press releases are really not difficult to put together and are important to send out regularly.

Comics Press Release and Interview Contacts

Table 11.1 lists 10 comic news and commentary sites that you'll want to send every press release to. These are also where you'll want to set up interviews about your webcomic. The e-mail addresses can be found at the URLs.

Table 11.1 Comic News and Commentary Sites

Name	Site	URL
Comic Book Resources News Wire	Comic Book Resources	www.comicbookresources.com/news/
Gary Tyrell	Fleen	www.fleen.com
Gigcast: The Webcomics Podcast	Gigcast	gigcast.nightgig.com
Jennifer Contino	The Pulse	www.comicon.com/pulse/
Matt Brady	Newsarama	www.newsarama.com
Matt Koelbl	Damn Good Comics	www.mrmyth.com
Robert Howard	Tangents	www.panel2panel.com
Comics Bulletin	Comics Bulletin	www.comicsbulletin.com
Tom Spurgeon	The Comics Reporter	www.comicsreporter.com
Xaviar Xerexes	ComixTalk	www.comixtalk.com

A Sample Press Release

The following is an example of a press release for one of our example web-comics, *The Drifter*. Pay special attention to the formatting.

THE DRIFTER: A HARD-BOILED TV DETECTIVE—IN COMICS!

March 15, 2008
For Immediate Release

Contact:
Steve Horton, co-creator, writer
steves_email@domain.com

Sam Romero, co-creator, artist
sams_email@domain.com

Today, the creative forces behind Graphic Smash webcomics *Grounded Angel* and *Edge the Devilhunter* team up for hard-hitting action on ComicSpace.com! Straight out of your fuzzy, rabbit-eared television set from 1982 comes *The Drifter*, an action hero from decades past. Pete Kincaid is forced to leave his private detective agency behind and hit the road, one step ahead of a shadowy organization, led by the G-Man, who wants him dead. With Kincaid is his beautiful assistant Jennifer Lancaster. Together they right wrongs for a price, but never stay too long in one place.

"I'm endlessly fascinated with American culture in the early 1980s, and I plan to have Kincaid visit as much of it as possible," says Steve Horton, writer and co-creator of *The Drifter*. "For example, in 1982, New York City was not a safe place at all. There's a lot of music and writing from the time that speaks to this effect, and I plan to throw Kincaid and Lancaster right in the middle of it.""I'm sort of going to be using *The Wire* as a source of inspiration," says Sam Romero, co-creator and artist of *The Drifter*. "I'm on the East Coast, Jersey to be precise, so I'm sure I can beat most other potential co-creators in terms of first-hand experience in inner-city decay and squalor. I must warn, I am an extreme left-ist as a result. I can offer plenty of first-hand insight into some of the inner workings of gentrification, illegal temp labor, machine politics, state corruption, police brutality, the welfare system, homelessness, racism, economic apartheid, and so on."

Along with being steeped in 1980s culture, *The Drifter* is also a deliberate homage to 1980s television police and detective dramas such as *Spenser: For Hire*, *Hardcastle & McCormick*, *Magnum P.I.*, and even *TJ Hooker*. The use of frequent guest stars, the choice of camera angles, and the chapter introductions are but two examples of this.

The Drifter is presented in 4:3 letterbox format, and a new episode premieres on www.ComicSpace.com every Friday.

An exclusive original chapter for *The Drifter* and its characters appears in the book *Webcomics 2.0*, by Horton and Romero, on sale now at bookstores everywhere from Course Technology PTR, a part of Cengage Learning.

About Smashout Comics: Smashout Comics (www.smashout.net) is an independent comics studio responsible for webcomics *Grounded Angel*, *The Drifter*, and *Gambling Souls*, the Image print comic *Strongarm*, and the how-to books *Webcomics 2.0* from Course PTR and *Professional Manga* from Focal Press.

Reviews

Submit your webcomic for review at a number of places that review such things. These webcomics reviews will be either positive or negative, depending on the reviewers' tastes. The good reviews can be quoted on your MySpace or ComicSpace page. The bad reviews are useful for constructive criticism. Either way, you'll get the word out about your webcomic.

Here are a few places that review webcomics You'll find contact information on the websites.

Fleen

Fleen (www.fleen.com) is the webcomics blog about webcomics. It's run by Gary Tyrell of Dumbrella, a comics collective that includes the popular Dinosaur Comics. Fleen is a great place to send webcomics news and press releases, as just about anything news-related involving webcomics gets coverage here.

ComixTalk

Run by Xaviar Xerexes, ComixTalk (www.comixtalk.com), formerly known as ComixPedia, is probably the most popular webcomics commentary site on the web. It's a must to send your stuff here.

Tangents

Tangents is a webcomics review blog run by Robert Howard, a longtime veteran of webcomics. Tangents appears on the blog collective Panel2Panel (www.panel2panel.com).

Damn Good Comics

Damn Good Comics (www.mrmyth.com) is another webcomics review blog that's been running since January 2006. It's run by Matt "Mr. Myth" Koelbl.

Interviews

Another good way to get the word out about your webcomic is to do an interview at one of the leading comics-related websites, many of which promote and support webcomics. The best way to do this is to simply fire off a professional e-mail to the contact person on the site. Talk about your webcomic a bit, link to some of the best pages, and request an interview.

If the site is interested, the interviewer will then send you several questions over e-mail, which you'll then answer. You'll be expected to provide several webcomics images for use on the site. It's also possible that the interviewer may opt to do the interview over the phone rather than e-mail.

Once the interview runs, it's a good idea to link to it from your website or social network page. A good interview can reveal a lot about yourself and your webcomic and gives the fans a greater connection to you and your work.

Out of the websites mentioned previously in this chapter, these run interviews: Newsarama, The Pulse, Comic Book Resources, Fleen, The Comics Reporter, and ComixTalk.

Low-Cost Promotion

Not all promotion is free. Some efforts require a little money on your part, but consider this an investment. Low-cost promotion done smartly will bring you readership, fans and popularity, and ultimately will make you more money. The important thing is not to go broke before that happens.

Store and Convention Signings

A signing is a planned and scheduled activity at a venue that requires you to show up, sit down at a table, and sign or sketch copies of your book.

Of course, doing a store or convention signing requires that there is something for the fans to sign. In the next chapter, you'll learn about creating collected editions of your webcomic. These books can be signed, and if you're the artist on the project, it's also nice to provide an individualized sketch on the inside front cover or first couple of pages.

Store Signings

Local comic shops, independent bookstores, and even big chain bookstores are all good venues for a store signing. Once you've got a bunch of copies of your collected edition in your hands, call up local comic shops and bookstores. Encourage them to order copies of your book from your publisher or from you (depending on the route you take to get published).

Keep in mind that if you self published and you convince a retailer to order directly from you, the retailer will want to order at a significant discount— 40% or higher. That's right around what it costs for you to order a copy of your own book, so you'll make no profit from this. However, this is a promotional activity that could bring you greater results in the future. If the store manages to sell a bunch of copies of your book at the signing and otherwise, you'll engender quite a bit of goodwill with this particular retailer. The retailer will be more inclined to schedule future signings and order copies of future books from you.

Some retailers will offer to sell your books on *consignment*. This means that you must provide them books free of charge, which they will then sell on their own time with their own shelf space. You and the retailer will then split profits on these sales, which may or may not make up for your costs.

If your webcomic book is published by someone else, it's probable that you'll get a stack of books from the print run for free (or deducted from your royalties). If you take this stack of books to a signing, you may be able to keep all of the money from the sales of those books. However, if you're signing copies that the store ordered itself, you'll have to work out some sort of arrangement. Some stores go 50/50 for their copies. Some will want to keep all the money and simply buy you a meal. Some won't even go that far, but if you sign a bunch of copies of your book, it's still worth your time. Again, this is a promotional opportunity, and even if you end up breaking even, or if it even costs you a bit of money for each copy that gets into the hands of a fan, it's worth it. You're sowing seeds, and, ultimately, this will help you in the long run.

Convention Signings

Though we go into far more detail on managing the convention trail in the next chapter, it's worth briefly mentioning it here. Just as in a store signing, the convention table is an excellent place to promote your webcomic. Often, someone's first exposure to a webcomic is through a show; the fan is inspired to visit your comic's website later and becomes a fan.

A Book Tour

Scheduling a series of signings at bookstores and conventions over a short span of time is called a book tour. If you promote the tour as an entity itself, then fans will be more likely to take your promotional effort more seriously. They see the work you're putting into it and figure you're in it for the long haul. Also, the more venues you hit during your tour, the more likely it is that your online fans will make it to one of them and get to meet you in person. This personal contact can really cement the fan–pro relationship.

Be sure and promote this book tour in the same online communities where you originally posted about your comic itself. Also, many comic blogs have built-in calendars, and a quick note to the blog master will get your book tour listed.

Doing a series of convention and bookstore appearances generally requires taking vacation time from a day job or not having a day job at all. Judicious use of weekends off and sick days can get you the time you need to hit local cons and bookstores, at least.

The Expense

The nice thing about bookstore and comic shop signings is that it's virtually cost free on your end. All you have to handle is travel costs to the venue and back. Picking places within driving distance is wise for this reason. It's probably not worth it to fly out for a store signing, but if you happen to be in town for a convention or other reason and can get from the convention to the signing and back easily, why not set one up?

A convention, however, can be expensive, as detailed in the next chapter. Reducing this cost is key to making it a worthwhile endeavor, hence it being mentioned in the low-cost section. The local, smaller shows will likely let you in free, but you'll also sell fewer books.. On the other hand, many find it difficult to sell books at megashows. Experiment with conventions of different sizes, and see what works best for you and your work. Once you find a convention that gives you steady business at your booth return to that convention the following year.

Buying Ad Space on Another Site

We've split up advertising in general into two chapters. In this chapter we'll talk a bit about ad buys, or purchasing ad space on another site that links to your webcomic. In the next chapter, we will cover ad sales, or selling ad space on your webcomic to someone else. Often, money from ad sales can be fed into ad buys, creating a system that supports itself.

Project Wonderful

The easiest to use and most efficient ad service out there is called Project Wonderful (www.projectwonderful.com). Created by webcomics creators and embraced by the webcomics community, Project Wonderful (Figure 11.4) allows people to bid on ad space, creating a situation where ads go for exactly what they are worth.

Before you check out the site, you'll want to create a couple of ads that represent your webcomic. The most useful shapes are 468×60 pixel banner ads and 160×600 skyscraper ads. Choose a striking single image from your comic that represents it well, such as a character. Consider creating an animated GIF. Make sure the ad incorporates your webcomic's logo.

Figure 11.4
The front page of
Project Wonderful.

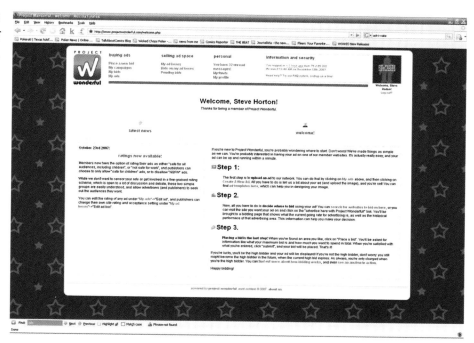

Sign up for an account on Project Wonderful and click on My Funds. Then add at least five bucks to your account with PayPal.

Create an Ad

Once your ad is all set and you've signed up for an account, click on My Ads, then Create Ad. You'll see the screen in Figure 11.5. Choose Graphical Ad and Banner or Skyscraper. The other ad sizes might be useful for you to create at some point, as well. Click Next.

You'll now be at the screen seen in Figure 11.6. Under URL, put in the Web address where your latest comic always appears. When in doubt, just put your comic's front page here.

When someone hovers over your ad with the mouse, a bit of text appears. The next box is where you'll tell Project Wonderful what that bit of text says.

Give the ad a nickname. Your webcomic's name is good. Click Next.

Figure 11.5
Choose the type of ad.

Figure 11.6
Enter your site's address.

On this page, as seen in Figure 11.7, choose Browse and select one of the ad images that you created previously. Then choose one of three ratings. C means the ad is safe for all audiences, including children. The middle rating is blank— the ad has no rating. The far right selection is NSFW, which stands for *not safe for work*. This is where the adults-only ads go.

Figure 11.7
Choose your ad's
image.

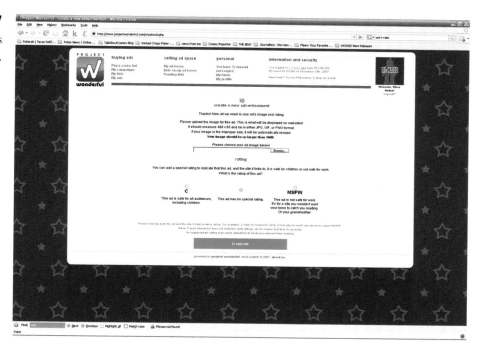

Then, click on Create Ad. Your ad is in the system, and now it's time to bid on space on another website.

Place a Bid

Click on Place a New Bid up at the top, as seen in Figure 11.8. Under Ad Sizes, deselect every choice except the one that represents the size of your ad. Under the Bidding selection on the far right, put in a range that represents how much you're spending on this. Fiddle with the other options if you wish, then click Search.

Once you've found a place where you want to advertise, click on Place Bid (Figure 11.9). This part works much like eBay. Put in a maximum bid, and the site will bid on your behalf up to that amount. You can also cap your bid at a certain amount. Click Place Bid.

Figure 11.8
Search for prospective sites.

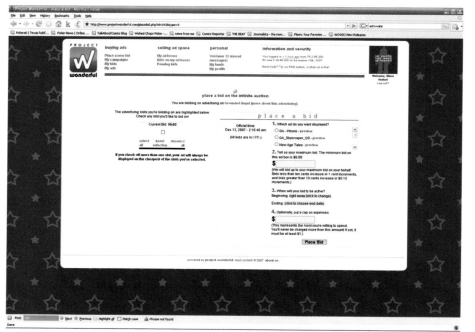

Figure 11.9
After choosing specific sites, place a bid.

Remember, your bid covers a single day of ad coverage. In other words, this is how much you're spending each day for your ad to appear on that site.

When you run out of money, your ad goes away. It's a good idea to spend a little bit to see how things work before graduating to the more expensive sites. It's also a good idea not to spend too much on this, because the ultimate goal is to get enough of a return on your advertising in the form of other income to make it a worthwhile expense.

Campaigns

You can also run your ad across several sites at once, without having to bid manually on each one. This is called a *campaign*. Click on My Campaigns and Start a New Campaign. These filtering options are the same as those with a standard bid. For a campaign, it's a good idea to filter toward several medium-traffic sites, weeding out the mega-popular (and expensive) sites. This will give you great coverage across a wide range of sites for your money.

The goal with filtering here is to click Search and have the results contain the sites you want as part of the campaign. Don't worry if there are a few in there that you dislike; you'll be able to filter them out later. When you have it narrowed down to what you like, click Create Campaign at the bottom of the screen. Then click Set Up This Campaign (Figure 11.10).

Pick start and end dates for the campaign. Put in the most you're willing to bid on any one single site within the campaign, the most you want to spend per day, and the most you want to spend overall, across all the sites.

Then select the ads you wish to use (Figure 11.11) and, under Exposure, fine-tune which sites are part of the campaign and which aren't.

The final box is highly important. This is the maximum number of high bids you want. According to the site's language, fewer high bids means a more focused campaign; more high bids gives you more exposure. Experiment with this and find out what works well for you.

If you're bidding on individual ads separately, you'll want to exclude them here. Then, click on Next to confirm and begin the campaign. Project Wonderful will then begin the process of automatically bidding on spots according to your criteria. You'll start seeing your ads appear on those sites within a couple of hours.

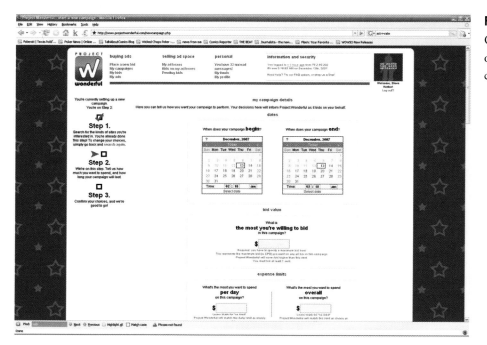

Figure 11.10
Choose your options for the campaign.

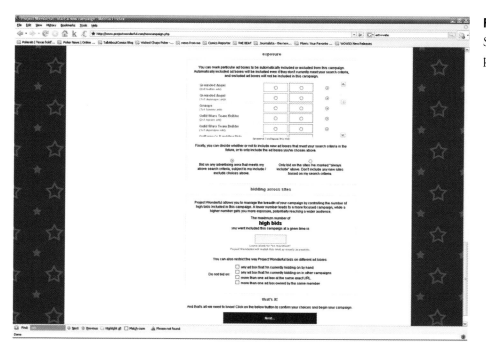

Figure 11.11
Select specific campaign ads.

Statistics

Project Wonderful has a wealth of statistics you can use to track how your ads are doing. You want to have the most page ad displays and clicks for the lowest cost. If you're spending a lot on an ad that nobody's seeing, dump it. If you're spending a small amount on an ad that's got tons of viewers and clicks, keep it. Eventually, the ads will start working their magic and bringing more people to the site, and that's when your superior content will, hopefully, keep them there. Right?

Webcomics 2.0 Interview: Project Wonderful

Ryan North is a true webcomics brainchild. He helped form the Dayfree Press webcomics collective. He created the popular dialogue-driven webcomic *Dinosaur Comics*. He created the webcomics content-tagging site OhNoRobot (www.ohnorobot.com). And he spearheaded a new approach to Web advertising that the webcomics community has latched on to. It's called Project Wonderful (www.projectwonderful.com). Here are some useful tips from North about maximizing your experience with this innovative site.

Webcomics 2.0: Can you tell me a little about how Project Wonderful works?

Ryan North: Sure! The basic idea is that, suppose you've got a website, and I've got an ad I want people to see. I can walk up and say "Steve, I am willing to pay up to $1 a day to have my ad on your site," and if I'm the high bidder, then my ad is displayed. Someone else can say "Forget Ryan, I'm willing to pay $2," and then their ad is displayed instead, and I'm only charged for the time I was the high bidder.

The end result is a marketplace that is responsive to both publishers and advertisers, transparent, profitable, and fair. Publishers like you can decide what kind of ads they want on their site and cancel them at any time, and advertisers have a powerful advertising search engine to find the kind of sites they want to advertise on.

Also, since Project Wonderful sells on the basis of time and not clicks or displays like other companies, issues like click fraud are eliminated entirely, which is great. Everyone involved can trust that they're not being ripped off.

WC20: It's been embraced by the webcomics community at large. Why do you think so many webcomics creators have opted to buy and sell ads on PW?

RN: I'd hope that it's because we offer a value that they can't find elsewhere. I think a lot of people are burned out on advertising companies that don't deliver on what they promise and don't give you the information you need to make an informed decision.

The issue is that ad companies are stuck between two conflicting goals: the highest profit for their publishers, and, at the same time, the cheapest price for their advertisers. Most of them negotiate this by not telling their advertisers what other advertisers have paid and are paying, and by not telling their publishers what the advertisers are paying them.

The end result is that the publishers get some money, but they don't know what percentage of the total it is. Advertisers feel uncertain about whether they're getting value for money. Project Wonderful gives you all the information you need, and you can see what other bidders have bid in the past before you commit.

I'd guess that's part of the reason. I hope it is, anyway. I also guess my online notoriety doesn't hurt.

WC20: The webcomics with the most traffic do seem to get a lot more money from ads. What are some things that a medium- or low-traffic webcomic can do to attract more lucrative bids?

RN: There are two main things they can do, and they both have to do with advertising placement.

What we've seen in some cases is a new publisher will put a single button ad on their site, and this ad will start earning them a few dollars a day. They think "Man, great! If one ad makes me $3, then 10 ads should make me $30," but unfortunately, it doesn't always work that way.

You can really picture it as a market, with classic supply and demand. If you've got three bidders on one ad, then demand is greater than supply; they're competing with each other and prices go up. But if you flood the market by covering your site with ads, anyone who wants a spot can get one for cheap.

The other side of that is placement. If you put an ad at the bottom of your page, that's much less valuable than putting it at the top. I think larger sites have been around longer and have more of a feel for this, while the smaller ones are experimenting more. I think that deciding on one or two ad slots with premium placement is the best thing a smaller webcomic can do to increase its bid value.

WC20: Do you think it's more important to stick with one ad size and shape until it works or to continue to try new formats and sizes?

RN: I think it really depends on the situation. There's nothing wrong with experimenting, and if the experiment fails, you can always go back to how it was before. But on the flip side, you can begin to alienate advertisers by constantly switching things around on them and forcing them to rebid. It hasn't really been an issue, though. I think most people are able to strike a balance between these pretty easily.

WC20: How important is it for a new webcomic to purchase ad space on other, more popular sites?

RN: Hah! As a guy behind Project Wonderful, I say it is absolutely critical 100% for reals. But as a webcomic author I can tell you that it takes time to build an audience. Advertising helps, but what helps best is having a few months of archives available for readers, a clean site design, a consistent update schedule, and the ability for readers to stay in touch with things like RSS feeds and forums.

You can certainly become a popular webcomic without spending a cent on advertising. But advertising can get you new readers, and that can speed that process along quite a bit.

Google AdWords

In the next chapter, we cover running Google AdSense ads on your site to make money. Here we're going to talk about the flip side—Google AdWords—which has to do with purchasing ad space on other sites.

First, go to adwords.google.com and sign up for an account. Pick the Starter Edition for now; you can mess around with the full Standard Edition at a later date. You'll now be at the screen seen in Figure 11.12.

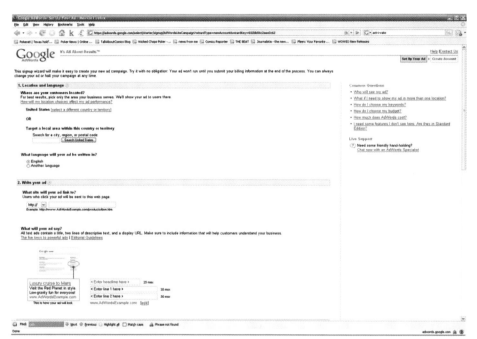

Figure 11.12
Enter your site's address and describe the site.

Put your website address under Write Your Ad and then compose three lines that describe your ad. The first should be the name of your comic, and the second two lines should be a good, attention-grabbing description of it.

Under Sample Keywords (Figure 11.13), add "webcomics," "web comics," and other keywords that clearly describe the nature of your webcomic and its elements. The keyword aspect to AdSense is critical. Choose your currency, and then add a monthly budget. Google recommends you start with $50/month; let's try that for one month. You might not spend it all.

Figure 11.13

Keywords are an important element of AdSense.

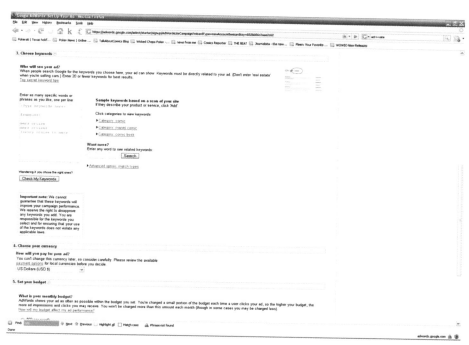

You'll probably want to uncheck the "extra help" box on the bottom of the screen, as this will free you from unwanted Google spam. Click Continue. You'll then be asked to enter your billing information.

After that, your ad will start showing up on sites that use specific comics-related keywords in their text. You'll be charged a specific amount each time someone clicks on one of your ads. The goal is to drive traffic toward your site and make it a good investment on your part.

With the advent of Project Wonderful, its graphical ads, and the greater control it provides over the campaign process, Google AdWords is no longer the number-one choice for buying ad space. Still, it's something to try out. It just might work for you.

A Final Note on Promotion

Though promotion is extremely important and should never be pushed aside, your promotion should never exceed your creativity. It's never wise to over-promote and underproduce. Your audience will quickly come to realize that you're all hype and no substance.

When it comes down to it, producing your comic should take priority. Never pass up regular updates in favor of promotion. If you're attending a show, commission some guest strips or work ahead so that a new comic hits the site on schedule in your absence. If you're spending a lot of time on your comic's MySpace page, make sure you've put in the work that day on the next comic. Nothing will drive fans away in droves faster than a lack of content. The best promotion works when there is something of value to promote. Balance is the key here—and when creativity and promotion are balanced, your webcomic will be the most successful it can be.

12

Making Money

And now, the big question: How do you make money from this thing? Ideally, you'd like to be paid back for all the time, effort, and emotional turmoil you've invested in your beloved webcomic. Though it's true that money-making opportunities increase in frequency and viability as your comic becomes more popular (see the previous chapter), there are still ways you can make a little money early in the life of your comic. And as your promotion efforts bear fruit and your comic starts to catch on, the money comes in as well. The trick is to be in the right place at the right time with your revenue-generating objects.

Revenue-Generating Objects

What is a revenue-generating object? It is a thing, separate and distinct but somehow related to your webcomic, that makes you money. There are four major revenue-generating objects for your webcomic: ads, merchandise, books, and downloadables.

Note that your webcomic is not one of the objects. However, it is your creativity in the comic's writing and art that fuels these objects and gives them life. If people like different aspects of your comic, whether it is snarky humor, sweeping adventure, or *shojo* manga romance, they are more likely to buy something based on that aspect to remind them of why they like you and your comic so much.

Advertising

One easy way to earn a few bucks is to run an ad banner on your site. Several of the webcomics collectives allow you to run your own banner ads and generate income from them. ComicSpace and DrunkDuck are two of these. Note that if you're running your webcomic on a blog service such as LiveJournal or a social networking service such as MySpace, you will not be able to do this. These sites run their own ads and do not allow users to run their own.

If you're hosting your webcomic on your own site, then obviously you can put ads wherever you want. Some webcomics, for ideological or aesthetic reasons, have chosen not to run any ads at all and to generate revenue in other ways. It's all about what's right for you.

There are two standard sizes of ads, though ads can come in many shapes and sizes. The most common type of ad is called a banner, and is usually 468×60 pixels in size. The second type of ad is a skyscraper. This vertical ad comes in 160×600 size.

Google AdSense

Yes, Google is everywhere. One tried and true method for ad banners is by using Google AdSense. Go to adsense.google.com and set up a banner ad there. Make sure it's a size and shape that will work on the site where your comics reside. Google's instructions are pretty straightforward. Once you've got the ad set up, the site will give you a line of code to paste into the appropriate location on your hosting site. This appropriate location is different for every site that allows ads; check with the site's instructions for details on where to drop this code.

ComicSpace has a specific area in its admin section just for ad banners.

DrunkDuck, however, requires you to paste the banner code in your site's HTML. Click on the Layout tab and then Raw HTML, and put the code just before this line:

```
<!--Comic Title Area-->
```

You'll know the banner ad works when it appears on your site. At first, you'll get public domain ads, but when Google becomes aware of your ad, you'll start seeing paid ads there. Every time someone clicks on them, you get some change. When your Google account hits $100, you can cash it out to your bank account.

Remember that, early in a strip's life, you'll be making only a few cents per click, so it'll take a while before you make your first $100. Get noticed, however, and you can bring in serious money from AdSense.

Project Wonderful

We first mentioned Project Wonderful in Chapter 11, "Promotion." That chapter went into detail about creating your own ad and buying ad space on another website. This time around, we'll be solving the other half of the equation: selling ad space.

After creating an account at www.projectwonderful.com, click on My Ad Boxes and create a new ad box. As with Google AdSense, make sure the size and shape work on your site. Typically, you'll choose Banner or Skyscraper and one row by one column. You'll receive the banner ad code. Click Next.

Then decide on ad approval and give it a nickname. Click Next again. Put in the URL where your comic is located and the name of the site, and give it a few tags and a description. Click on Create Ad Box, and then click on Ad Box Settings Page. You will now see the code that you'll need to paste in the appropriate place on your site. (See the "Google AdSense" section earlier in this chapter for the correct spot on DrunkDuck.)

Now other sites will bid on ad placement, and you'll get paid based on their bids, regardless of who actually clicks on the ad. Bidders will be able to see the traffic on your site, and webcomics with more traffic naturally get higher bids on their ads.

Project Wonderful requires only $10 in your account in order to withdraw. You can either put that money directly toward buying ads via Project Wonderful or cash it out to your bank account. It's your choice.

There are many strategies when selling ad space on Project Wonderful. Experiment with multiple button-size ads. If many buttons are going toward free or 1-cent ads, reduce the number of buttons. Experiment with more than one banner or more than one skyscraper. It's possible that more than one of these types on your page will still lead to higher values and more money for you.

Merchandise

There are three primary ways of going about creating webcomics-related merchandise.

Merchandise: Print on Demand

The easy way is simply to go to a website such as www.spreadshirt.com, www.zazzle.com, or www.cafepress.com and create the T-shirt, coffee mug, or other item using the built-in interface. You can then link to your creations from your comic. The downside to using these services, called *print-on-demand* (POD), is that items are created only after someone orders it, giving you only a tiny profit per item. T-shirts and other items tend to be on the expensive side. It's asking a lot for a fan to pay $20 or more for a T-shirt. The upside of this method is that it's easy and relatively painless to set up, and requires no risk on your part.

Presale

The other way is to talk to a T-shirt screen printer or other item manufacturer about setting up a small print run just for you. The size of this print run is determined by preorders. You then ask your fans to preorder an item from you, often at a significantly cheaper price than print on demand.

Set a preorder deadline, and while you're waiting for the preorder deadline to pass, talk to the printer and provide all the files they will need. Communicate the deadline with them.

When you have enough preorders, you take the money to the shop, which then creates them all and sends them to you. It's then your job to pack and ship those items. The upside is price—this way, you can sell items for reasonable prices. The drawback is twofold: If you don't get enough preorders, the shop might not be able to make the items at all. Also, fans might have to wait several weeks from preorder to receiving the item.

For T-shirts, Brunetto Shirts at www.brunettoshirts.com is used by many webcomics creators and is one of the most reputable online screen print companies out there. Give them a try. You can also try a local screen printer to save on shipping costs, thus bringing down the price for the fans.

Investment

The third way is to just bite the bullet and order a bunch of custom-made items yourself from a printer or shop, preferably one in your city. (Ordering this way from a POD company is not recommended because they offer creators only a tiny discount.) Again, if you're doing a T-shirt, you're going to want to look for a screen printer. You're not worrying about preorders, but this requires an initial investment on your part that you might not get back for awhile, if at all. Since this chapter is on making money and not spending it, this method is recommended when your strip is already pulling in a bit of dough that you can re-invest in it. The big upside is that fans can buy an item cheap and receive it right away, directly from you. The downside, as we mentioned, is the cost. This is the preferred method, though, when planning to attend a show, as we'll discuss later in the chapter.

As mentioned above, www.brunettoshirts.com is a good place to try for a T-shirt investment.

What to Put on a T-Shirt?

The thing about T-shirts, many webcomics creators have found, is that the biggest selling shirts have almost nothing to do with the comic itself. Instead, through the course of writing the strip, sometimes creators come up with witty sayings or other imagery that would make people laugh if it were on a shirt. Order of the Stick's "Your d12 Cries Itself to Sleep" shirt is one example. Its humor usually is related to the subject matter of the comic, but often it doesn't feature any comic characters or situations at all.

The other types of shirts are those featuring characters from the strip. Either the characters simply appear on the shirt in a dynamic pose, or it's a re-creation of a quote or fan-favorite scene from the comic.

It's good to experiment with different types of shirts and find out what your readers respond to.

Every shirt manufacturer is going to want a high-resolution file in a specific format, usually PNG or TIF. It has to look good on a shirt, so it might be a good idea to fire up one of the POD sites listed above, just to create a shirt on the Web and see how it might look in real life. Don't actually go through with creating the shirt, though—you're just using the POD site to assist you visually.

The Webcomics 2.0 Interview: Brunetto T-shirts

A favorite among webcomics creators, Brunetto T-shirts (www.brunet-totshirts.com) is a screen-printing service that accepts preorders and short print runs from creators. They are not a print-on-demand service, so to use Brunetto or another screen printer requires collecting preorders from customers (see the "Presale" section in this chapter).

The interviewee is Kurt Brunetto, owner of Brunetto T-shirts.

Webcomics 2.0: Which webcomics first got turned on to Brunetto T-shirts as a screen printing source?

Kurt Brunetto: I knew Rich Stevens of Diesel Sweeties. I started printing for Diesel Sweeties and explodingdog back in 2000.

WC20: Why do you think so many webcomics creators have latched on to your service?

KB: Most are recommended from other webcomics. I think if I do a quality job at a good price, people will be happy.

WC20: How does your short print-run service compare with a print-on-demand service such as, say, Cafepress?

KB: [Creators] can make more money per shirt if they order from me and do the order processing themselves.

Also, the quality is better since it's screen printed instead of heat press designs.

WC20: When a creator prefers to do a preorder to collect funds from interested fans, what kind of files do you need from the creator in the meantime?

KB: If they send me the art beforehand, I can have the screens made for when the preorder is done. It helps get the shirts to the customers faster.

WC20: Is there a crunch time before big conventions, when many creators want to place large orders?

KB: Yes; Comic-Con International: San Diego is in July, so June is pretty busy. November is pretty busy, too, because of Christmas.

Merchandise Other Than Shirts

Merchandise to consider other than T-shirts include postcards, posters, and art prints. These items are terrific for conventions, as we'll get into later in the chapter. Postcards are usually an investment and are given away free; they increase awareness of your book and are more of a promotional tool than anything. Posters and art prints are usually sold and are a great way to show off a webcomic that has great art.

Books

As with merchandise, there are a few different ways to go with collected editions based on your webcomics. Before considering a book, though, you've got to build up enough of an archive to justify one. Assume that a book contains about 180 pages of material. If your comic is once a week, that means you'll be doing a book every 3.5 years or so. Three times a week means that you'll have 156 strips by year's end—you can put all that into one book with some extras and call it a day. If your strip is five times a week, that means each book will contain about 8 months of material or so. No matter how you look at it, you'll need to have your webcomic going for a while before it'll be ready to collect.

Books: Print on Demand

The first method is going with a book print-on-demand service, such as www.lulu.com. Once you've got the book prepared using Lulu's step by step tutorial, fans can sign on to Lulu's website or even click a button from your site to order your book. Lulu will print one up and mail it out. The nice thing about Lulu specifically is that prices for book collections end up being very similar to how a book would be priced at a traditional book store, and you get a few bucks for each book sold. The downside is that your book will be available to order only online. Print-on-demand books rarely appear in real-life bookstores because they have the vanity press stigma attached to them. In other words, big bookstores feel that a publisher and editor are required in the process for them to carry your book.

Also consider Amazon.com's BookSurge service. It works similar to Lulu's but has the advantage of instant placement on Amazon, where many eyeballs will see it.

The Webcomics 2.0 Interview: Lulu

Lulu (www.lulu.com) is a print-on-demand service that specializes in comic book collected editions, also known as trade paperbacks or graphic novels. Many webcomics creators use Lulu to make their collected editions, and the fans have an easy way to order books. Creators can also self-order copies this way to take to conventions. Lulu has been around for a long time and has earned a lot of respect in the industry.

The interviewee is Nick Popio, community specialist for Lulu.

Webcomics 2.0: How has the response been for webcomics creators who wish to make collected editions of their work?

Nick Popio: So far, the response has been really good. I think fans of webcomics like being able to have a collection they can read, and they get an opportunity to support the creator at the same time. It may seem contrary to a lot of other business models, because people are paying for something they can get for free, but many creators develop relationships with their readers that are a lot closer than in other settings (traditionally published comics, for example). As a result, you see readers who will happily purchase content they have access to for free because in exchange they get a physical copy (which is something I think many people still want), and they know they are supporting the creator directly.

WC20: What if the webcomic is created in a non-standard size, taking advantage of the Web as a canvas? Have you been able to accommodate non-standard sizes for collections?

NP: Currently, we offer a wide-variety of sizes for collections. They range from 4.25×6.875 to 8.5×11, and we offer different formats like landscape and square. Of course, there are going to be sizes we can't accommodate, because the images weren't made to be put into a book. I would suggest though that with creativity, even those non-standard sizes could be formatted in ways that make unique use of our sizes. Of course, there is also the option of not doing a book and doing a series of prints or framed art through our site as well.

WC20: Why would webcomic creators go with your service as opposed to investing in a print run at a traditional printer?

NP: It's really about what they are hoping to accomplish. One of the big drawbacks to a traditional printer is that there is usually a large upfront cost to the creator. With Lulu, there is no upfront cost, and the only time the creator has to spend any money is if he orders copies of his book for himself or to take to a convention. Another highlight of Lulu is that we base our pricing on an 80/20 split of the royalties. The creator sets his own royalty after the base price is determined ($4.53 plus two cents a page for black and white or 15 cents a page for color), and we then add 20% to that, which is our cut.

The creator can make a dollar per book, or he can make 10 dollars; it's whatever he wants. After he has priced his book, he can link directly to the content from his website using our *Buy Now* buttons or our mini-storefront widget, and fans can purchase from us. On top of all that, the creator keeps all of the rights to his work. With that level of flexibility, he really has very little to lose in trying Lulu.com.

WC20: How important is it that creators save high-res versions of their webcomics separately?

NP: I would say it's very valuable and will save a lot of time for them if they ever want to create a physical collection of their work. You want to make sure you have easy access to images that can be printed and will look good.

WC20: Is there anything else a webcomics creator needs to keep in mind when creating, to make the eventual print process at Lulu easier?

NP: The biggest thing is making sure you have copies of your images that are high enough quality for printing. Ideally, you should know what kind of layout and formatting you want to use so that you can optimize your images for that process. The easiest and most effective way to publish on Lulu.com is to get your book ready and then make it into a PDF, so you may want to look into ways to create a PDF, but it is not required for upload. We accept most standard digital formats, and you can always check our list of accepted formats here at http://www.lulu.com/en/help/index.php?fSymbol=upload_filetypes. The publishing wizard walks you through the whole process and contains lots of contextual help.

We also offer 24/7 live chat help, so even if you're working late, you can still get the answers you need. We try to make the process as easy as possible for the creator, so that fans can order the book as soon as possible.

Investing in a Print Run

As with investing in a T-shirt run, this method costs money. There are several printers out there, such as Brenner, that will accept small book runs of a thousand copies or so. You're looking at an investment of $1,000 or more for something like that, though. This is something to think about when your comic is doing really well, and you want to earn a greater profit per book compared to POD. It is also something to consider when you're attending a series of conventions and have a long lead time, as printers can take a long time to get set up, print, and get you your books, especially during peak convention season when the major publishers have priority.

Signing with a Publisher

Many webcomics creators have submitted their work to a print comics publisher and been accepted. Image/Shadowline publishes *The Surreal Adventures of Edgar Allen Poo* as a comic book, which appears on the webcomics collective The Chemistry Set. DC's CMX imprint publishes digest collections of *Megatokyo*, one of the most popular webcomics. Dark Horse Comics publishes book collections of *Penny Arcade*, one of the Web's most popular webcomics.

That's not to say that you have to be insanely popular to get published. Having a good run of quality work can be enough. The nice part is that it doesn't matter if the publishers pay you on the front end (a page rate) or on the back end (depending on sales). The work's already completed for the Web, so it's not as if you're drawing it as you go. It takes very little work to put together files suitable for publication. It's worth repeating the importance of saving files in high resolution, even though you'll use low-res for the Web. This high-res version is what you'll need for print.

Preparing for Print

This is where your high-resolution, print-ready webcomic prepared in Chapter 9, "The Art," really comes in handy. With these high-res files, getting your webcomic set up for a book is a snap.

One thing you'll need to create is a cover. Some creators make an entirely new image for the cover. Others take a really snappy image from an existing comic's panel and reuse it for the cover. Note that if your comic is black and white, this image will have to be color, so find someone good to color it for you.

You'll also need to create a logo for the cover if your webcomic doesn't have one already. Again, it might help to solicit outside help for this. Make sure the logo is easy to understand and readable from a distance.

After the cover is done, simply collect your high-res files in a format that the printer wants. The two most common are TIF and PNG, and your image program will let you convert between them if necessary. Resolution will be around 400 dpi. You will then likely have to upload the image files to the printer's site using either their website or FTP. Website uploading is straightforward enough, but for FTP you'll want to read up on how to use it. See the sidebar in Chapter 10, "What is FTP?" for details on using FTP.

Once you've transferred the files, the printer you're using will explain how to go from there. You'll likely be examining proofs, or printer-ready files. Make sure the proofs are free of errors, as that's the last step before your book is printed up and delivered to you.

Downloadables

One other way to make money from a webcomic is to offer it in another form. If a fan can download a collected run of webcomics in a package, he can read them offline at his leisure. These downloadable packages come in two formats: PDF and CBR.

PDF

Portable Document Format (PDF) is a standard used by Adobe for documents that are viewable in many environments. What that means to you is that you'll need to convert your images into PDF. To do this, you'll need to own a copy of Adobe Acrobat 8 Standard. You can find a copy of this on eBay for about $60, and you'll be able to create a PDF with ease. Free PDF creation utilities are available, but none of them work as well as the real deal.

A couple of websites will let you publish your PDF with them. This PDF will be either sold or given away, and you'll get a cut for each download.

The three major sites that do this are DriveThruComics, Wowio, and Clickwheel. See the interview sidebars for more details on these companies.

You can also offer the PDF for download free on your own site, if you wish, though none of the above companies will let you do this if you're with them.

Webcomics 2.0 Interview: DriveThruComics

DriveThruComics (www.drivethrucomics.com) is a spinoff of the popular site DriveThruRPG, which allows paper-and-pencil RPG fans to purchase and download legal PDFs of their favorite RPG modules. This site has kept many RPG companies in business by giving them another avenue to get their product to gamers. DriveThruComics uses the same principle: For a small fee, comic book fans can download PDF comics from many different publishers, including webcomics publishers.

The interviewee is Steve Wieck, publisher relations and marketing for DriveThruComics.com.

Webcomics 2.0: The prospect of offering comic books as digital PDF downloads has angered some retailers. How do you respond to that?

Steve Wieck: Download comics are here to stay. The question is not if download comics will exist; they already do. The question is how they exist: legally or illegally.

The comic market as a whole, even retailers included, is benefited when readers have the option to download titles at a fair price, rather than illegally from piracy sites. If readers who desire to get their comics digitally have no legal option, then they become more compelled to try the illegal file-sharing route to get their titles. That doesn't help anyone in the market, ultimately not even the consumer. Associating a fair value to comic content and asking readers to make the right choice maintains the value prospect of comics.

Will local comic shops lose some sales to download comics? Yes, they already do, thanks to piracy. Download comics can also benefit local comic shops in less obvious ways, though. For example, iTunes showed in music, and our roleplaying game download sites (DriveThruRPG and RPGNow) have also shown that the convenience and availability of downloads re-engages older demographics who had previously stopped buying much music or roleplaying games. Older gamers just didn't make it to the game shop as often and drifted out of the hobby. Now that they have become reengaged in purchasing games, they're also going back and buying in print as well.

Unlike music where the downloaded MP3 is the preferred medium for the user (better than buying a CD that they need to burn into their computer anyway), comics and roleplaying games are still generally preferred in print format. When a former comic collector or gamer gets reengaged by the download medium, their purchases drift back into print.

WC20: Why PDF and not a security-free format such as CBR?

SW: User convenience is of paramount importance to us. Everyone has a PDF reader on their computer already; not so with CBR. Yes, there are free CBR readers available, but you are still putting a roadblock in front of the user for first use. PDFs are ubiquitous and well known to most computer users. CBR requires some education to begin to use.

Our PDFs have a watermarked security feature that does not inhibit the reader from enjoying the comics. There is no-DRM type security on our downloadable comics; readers just download the PDFs, open them, and enjoy.

Of lesser concern is that we have tools on our site that automatically generate previews and the watermarking security based on PDF files, not CBR. While others may have differing opinions, we don't yet find that the reading experience is significantly better or worse with PDF versus CBR.

WC20: Many of your downloads began at $1.99, but many of them are settling down at $0.99. How do you feel about 99 cents becoming a de facto standard for downloadable content such as comics?

SW: I think it's too early to tell what the right price of download comics will be. We're still in the early market development stages. I agree with Steve Jobs that offering customers a standardized price is a very attractive thing, but I don't think that can work for comics where the market has a wide variety of formats of sizes or work.

WC20: Do you see some of the major publishers offering their products for download in the near future?

SW: Naturally we've made a case with each of the majors as to why we think it's a good idea for them to offer download titles via DriveThruComics. So far, the majors are all pursuing their own models.

So far, their approaches have focused on offering free downloads as marketing tools. That's certainly a smart move, but it's just the tip of the iceberg of the potential for download comics. They are completely missing the revenue side.

It is hard for me to fathom why every comic ever printed from the majors, at least the issues not hog tied by legal issues, is not already available for legal download. Comic publishers are missing a gold mine by not adding the revenue side of download comics to the marketing side of it that they are already doing. We will continue to preach the virtues and hope that more will take advantage. When it happens, it will benefit the comics market in a way that will approach the positive impact of the manga invasion of the past decade.

WC20: Say someone wanted to create a webcomic and publish it online and as a downloadable PDF, but offer no initial print version. Is that a good business model?

SW: Being purely digital to start is a great business model. Ask any small press creator about the difficulties of getting noticed in the print market distribution channels. The cost of print runs, shipping, and marketing can become a sizeable and high-risk investment.

That said, most of the webcomic creators I know are not able to make their webcomic into a living, but they can build up a large fan base online. The key is to then "monetize" that fan base they create online. The PayPal donation box, CafePress bling, and Project Wonderful ads are fine, but they seldom pay enough to make the comic creation a full-time gig.

The emerging trend seems to be to build up the audience via webcomics and then try to make a living by selling that audience printed collections, and now download collections as well. For example, Tarol Hunt, who creates the *Goblins!* webcomic (www.goblinscomic.com) has worked with DriveThruComics to offer a compilation of the comics as a download. By including a chapter of bonus material and coloring some early black-and-white strips, Tarol's compilation offered fans value added at a very fair price. Fans are willing to support their favorite webcomics, but it is an easier decision for most fans to support through a purchase than through straight donation.

Webcomics 2.0 Interview: Wowio

Wowio (www.wowio.com), the free PDF download site, had already been around for several months before it radically changed its business plan. Thanks to sponsorship by Verizon, CareerBuilder and others, the company decided to pay creators 50 cents for each download of its free PDFs, including comics. The comics population has exploded on the site since then, with some comics, including collected webcomics, pulling in five figures of quarterly income for their creators.

The interviewee is Mike Miller, authorized representative of Wowio.

WC20: WOWIO is one of the few places where webcomic print collections and print comic books coexist. How do you feel about that?

Mike Miller: I think it's fantastic. The two worlds are so vastly different. Where you'll see primarily 30+ white men in comic-book stores buying print comics, you will find 70–80% of webcomics readers under the age of 35 of both genders and all races (according to Wowio demographics). The webcomics readers are the next generation of comics fans, and they'll never step foot into a comic book store, but here on Wowio, they can access hundreds of different print comics available legally on the Web for the first time. It's a great way to introduce webcomic readers to more traditional comics, even if they still never buy a printed book. As a print comic fan, I hope they do, but at least they still don't have to, and it's all still free.

WC20: What are some ways that a new webcomic going the Wowio route can increase the downloads and make more money?

MM: If a new webcomic [creator] who has a small fan base can turn every new fan into a reader of his books on Wowio.com, he gets paid for each download. Otherwise, he is reliant on Google ads or other ads like Project Wonderful, or he's begging for donations. None of those options make a new webcomic [creator] much money at all. But on Wowio, if they direct those fans to download the books for free, they still get paid for each download. I know it's redundant, but the point is important enough to repeat. There is basically no valid source of revenue for new webcomics, no matter how great they are, unless they're on a service like Wowio. And, to date, the only service like Wowio is Wowio.

WC20: It's possible that a prospective print publisher might balk at a webcomic appearing as an e-book first. Have you heard of this situation coming up?

MM: As former executive director at Alias Comics, I looked at the fan base of the popular webcomic *Penny and Aggie* and decided to offer them a chance to see their comic in print. I had hoped their webcomic fan base could be translated into print-comic sales. It didn't. That's not to say that it couldn't, but it's as I described above—the webcomics fans are the new generation. They sit in front of their computers for seven hours a day, reading and watching stuff for free. What is their incentive to go out of their way to a comic book store half an hour away and pay three bucks for something they can read in five minutes? These people are not collectors. They don't want 200 long boxes sitting in their garage collecting dust. They want to read good content for free. And that's what Wowio allows them.

Back to the question: Should publishers balk at e-books? No. Frankly, most of the print comics audience has never bothered reading a comic online unless it was a preview or something of the sort. And if it's a web-comic first, there's little difference between that and an e-book, aside from format. The print folks will still buy the print version, and the Web folks will still read the Web version. Thus far there has been very little crossbreeding.

WC20: Why would a webcomic creator choose this route for collections over a route that might take away some rights to the work in exchange for benefits?

MM: I'm not sure what benefits you're talking about, but Wowio is not an exclusive publisher of e-books. We're only exclusive in our particular model. Many of our publishers have their books not only on Wowio, but on DriveThruComics, Pullbox, or Lulu. We're just one more outlet, but one that offers e-books to its readers for free, while still paying the publisher. Thus far, it has been extraordinarily successful, as many of our publishers can attest.

WC20: What can you tell me about new features or improvements that will benefit comics on Wowio over the next several months?

MM: I can't give you any specifics, but we are and will always be a work in progress. Wowio is always trying to better itself, as any business should. We're always considering ways we can improve our ease and breadth of use and make it as comfortable as possible for new readers to enjoy the Wowio experience. We are always open to suggestions as well on how folks think we might be able to better serve the e-book and e-comic community.

CBR/CBZ

The CBR/CBZ format is a collection of JPGs of your comic, compressed with a RAR or ZIP utility, respectively, and then renamed so that the extension reads .cbr or .cbz instead of .rar or .zip. The file can then be read by many popular comic reader utilities such as CDisplay. People use CDisplay to read scans of print comics, so naturally it works well for reading a digital collection of your webcomic. Though selling your CBR/CBZ is possible, it's better to offer it as a free alternative to browsing your archives, helping your strip's traffic and popularity, and making money that way.

Comics for Mobile Devices

It's possible to reformat your webcomic so it's suitable for a mobile device, such as an iPod, iPhone, Nintendo DS, or other mobile phone or PDA. This is a smart move. In Japan, so many people read manga on cell phones that it's putting a serious dent in the print manga industry. The thing to remember here is that mobile devices have a much lower resolution than print. Each device is going to need a different size panel to match to it.

Enter Clickwheel (www.clickwheel.net). This site, owned by Rebellion/2000AD of *Judge Dredd* fame, allows you to create and format your comics specifically for the iPod and iPhone. This site normally doesn't pay its creators. However, it does sponsor a certain number of webcomics, and these webcomics get paid. It's a good idea to get set up on Clickwheel. It's free, and you don't even need an Apple device to see how it'll look. If they like you, they'll say so. See the interview for more on these guys.

The other major player in this field is GoComics (www.GoComics.com), a site owned by Universal Press Syndicate. They look for the brightest and the best comics and turn them into mobile phone wonders. You'll have to contact them and submit samples. They look for quality and a certain level of family-friendliness. Your comic doesn't have to be cute animals, but it'll have to go easy on the violence and sex. There's some pretty good money in it if GoComics signs you on. There's an interview with GoComics later in this chapter.

Webcomics 2.0 Interview: Clickwheel

One of the first non-Japanese companies to explore the comics on mobile devices space, Clickwheel (www.clickwheel.net) was recently purchased by Rebellion/2000AD, the UK comics juggernaut, giving it a much broader reach into the market. The site focuses on Apple's products, such as the iPhone and iPod, and has emulators that allow creators to see exactly how their comic will look on those devices.

The interviewee is Tim Demeter, editor-in-chief of Clickwheel.

WC20: Tell me about Clickwheel.

Tim Demeter: Clickwheel is the first site dedicated to distributing comics to the iPod and now the iPhone via Clickwheel.net as well as the iTunes store. We offer everything a creator needs to get his comic from his desktop to a user's iPod, from online tools to how-to sections ranging from the casual user to the creator who really wants to press the limits of this new way of making and reading comics.

The site was founded in 2005 by Will Simons, who serves as the site's creative director. After the first year, Clickwheel began to outgrow itself, so in 2006, Will contacted Jason Kingsley, the CEO of Rebellion, another Oxford-based company. Within a few months, a deal had been struck for Rebellion to buy Clickwheel.

WC20: The site is now owned by Rebellion/2000AD. What does this mean for Clickwheel?

Rebellion gives Clickwheel the luxury of both capital and direction from one of the most successful independent video game studios out there.

Due to their help, we at Clickwheel are now able to do our jobs much more effectively and are supported by some truly brilliant folk.

Rebellion's ownership of UK comic publisher 2000AD also gives us access to thousands of unique properties, including such notable creations as *Judge Dredd*, as well as the guidance of a publisher who has worked with creators like Alan Moore, Grant Morrison, and Warren Ellis.

We are working on a number of collaborative efforts with 2000AD and have a number of the UK's finest comics available for download already.

WC20: What are some of the new features the site has now?

TD: In addition to our automated upload and download functions, as well as our ability to port comics to iTunes automatically, Clickwheel.net now features advanced bookmarking and "favoriting" tools to help users keep track of their favorite comics, as well as a new tag-based search tool to help them browse for new favorites.

We've also added community features such as creator profiles, a forum both to help fans connect with their favorite creators and allow those creators to drive traffic to their personal site, store, blog, or whatnot.

Clickwheel has also launched a trailer section that allows comic creators to upload trailers or previews of their comics for distribution via Clickwheel. Our goal is to organize as many comic trailers as possible in one quickly searchable, easily browsed area, giving fans a one-stop spot to see what's coming from their favorite creators and helping creators promote their projects to the iPod generation.

The iPhone has been a motivator in many of our new efforts, as its dynamic interface allows a huge amount of flexibility both in reading and creating mobile comics. We keep our creators up to date on the latest recommendations from Apple and are continually optimizing our features to take advantage of the latest technology. For those who do not have access to an iPhone, we've developed a Push Comics player that allows users to simulate the iPhone's interface from their computers. This allows creators to test out potential iPhone comics without owning one, as well as allowing readers to enjoy some of Clickwheel's exclusive iPhone content from their personal computers.

WC20: How does one go about getting onto Clickwheel? Does the comic have to be good? Are there restrictions on content?

TD: Clickwheel is primarily an online service provider and is open to any creator with a comic. We do go the extra mile to feature work we think is of exceptional effort, as I believe that is only fair, but we encourage all creators to take advantage of our unique tools.

The only content we restrict is material that would be considered "adult." Granted, this can be a fine line, but I work with creators on a case-by-case basis to ensure that the creator is not sacrificing his storytelling intentions, but still adhere to a certain standard of decency.

WC20: Some creators are paid for being on the site? How does this work?

TD: We commission exclusive work on a project-by-project basis, which is to say we commission a specific piece from a specific creator/creative team, and I negotiate an agreed upon length and rate for the entire project or set a page/frame rate.

The exact amount, like any other job, is commensurate with the size of the workload and the experience of the freelancer.

We do have non-exclusive work on the site as well, but we currently pay only for exclusive work, and while the site is open to all, the exclusive work is chosen by the editor, just like any comic company.

The freelance commissions are exclusive for six months but include no rights acquisition. We respect our creator's rights to their own intellectual properties.

Webcomics 2.0 Interview: GoComics

GoComics (www.GoComics.com) is a company and website owned by Universal Press Syndicate. In the past, Universal Press generally concerned itself with newspaper comics. In today's push toward the Web for comics, the syndicate is making a push as well toward comics on mobile devices. Enter GoComics.

The interviewee is Harold Sipe, mobile product manager for Uclick/GoComics.

WC20: How does one go about repurposing a webcomic, newspaper comic, or print comic for a cell phone?

Harold Sipe: We have different approaches for each format. Newspaper comics probably have the easiest time of it from a formatting standpoint. Uclick is the sister company of Universal Press Syndicate, so we have been presenting syndicated newspaper strips on the Web for years. Most of these strips are three or four panels; the graphics are fairly high contrast, and the lettering fairly large by comic book standards. These strips come almost ready-made for mobile in that they are created with the idea of reduction that is necessary for presentation in today's newspapers. Beyond setting the threshold for the minimum reduction, while keeping in mind the presentation of the work and reader experience, there is little formatting involved.

Most webcomics we currently work with are done in the "newspaper strip" format. Offhand, I am thinking of *PvP* and *The Norm*. Again, there is not a lot of formatting involved. Some titles employ what I call the "half-page" format. *Too Much Coffee Man* is a good example of this; it is the format the new Zuda Comics program from DC Comics is mostly focusing on. These titles are a bit more involved. Right now, on most American handsets we are restricted to a panel-by-panel slideshow presentation. We then create graphic files of each panel in the strip. It is worth noting we always go back to the creators with these formatted files for approval and to make sure we are conveying as much of the reading experience as possible in this format.

Comic books are the most challenging. It is not enough to just present the books panel-by-panel, since there are many storytelling conventions you have to consider. We are really lucky to have such a huge community of comics creators here in Kansas City. We have sought these folks out to consult and, in some cases, help with the design work of mobile comic book formatting. We have developed a lot of standards for how to deal with splash pages, how to keep the tension built in a whole page, how to deal with captions and word balloons, and so on. Again, we also go back to the creators as much as possible to ensure that we are conveying the correct intention of each page.

WC20: What kinds of webcomics are you looking for? Any specific genre, type, or age range?

HS: I always like to think of comics in general as a big tent. The form can speak to lots of situations and genres. I think a lot of the success that manga has enjoyed in Japan is directly due to the diversity of subject matter. In most cases the mobile comics readers are marketed to a user directly on his phone, and odds are, these folks are not already regular comics readers. Because of this, we try to offer a wide variety of quality material to appeal to as many users as possible.

Most of the titles in our mobile readers skew "younger" than a lot of our traditional syndicated comic strips, which I think is expected when you start working with comic book and manga titles. We have learned that a large number of mobile content users are women, so we do keep things like that in mind when we are looking at content. Between the Virgin Comics titles, *TokyoPop* (Original English Language) manga, and newer "indie" titles like *Foxymoron* and *Disquietville*, we really do try and capture as much of the potential audience as possible.

There are a few content issues we have to be careful of on account of the phone companies, but these are mainly language issues and keeping an eye on violence.

WC20: Does the creator have to do any redrawing or relettering to make it readable?

HS: We don't ask the creators to do any of this work for mobile formatting. We take care of all the design and production work when we are preparing the material for cell phones. While we do have to adjust the lettering in most cases, we try very hard not to alter or edit the art in any way. Working with comic book artists on most of the design work helps because they are so sensitive to the material.

WC20: With the advent of the iPhone, how has the demand for mobile comics been affected?

HS: Well, in the short term I don't see any effect on demand. Much like in the world of personal computers, Apple represents a small percentage of overall handsets. When competitors start following suit and we all are walking around with portable wi-fi Internet devices—that is when it will become a very different ballgame. As the limited version of the Internet that mobile users know now goes away, we will really be looking at cross-platform publishing—where a user can read comics on his PC, his phone, and likely other mobile devices and gaming platforms.

WC20: Reading manga on cell phones in Japan is extraordinarily popular. Do you foresee U.S. mobile comics reaching that level?

HS: Manga in Japan, whether on mobile or in print, is more widely read and highly regarded than comics are here in the U.S. Having said that, the American public is being exposed to comics through movie adaptations and the Internet, and the quality is improving, so that perception of comics may be changing. The other issue we have here in the U.S. is that the phones are "dumb" compared to the devices used in Japan. That, too, is changing, albeit very slowly.

I love comics, I believe in them. I firmly believe that if we, GoComics, or any other new media publisher can put a compelling reading experience in front of users, we can win them over. It's an interesting time to be looking at these issues, as Web and mobile converge. Will it be as big here as in Japan? I think if the titles are there and we can put a good user experience in front of consumers, we can make a real run of it.

Revenue-Generating Locations

Now that you have merchandise, books, and downloadables, where does this stuff go in order to make money? There are two key locations where you need to promote and support your items in order to make your strip some cash and keep your Ramen noodles flowing and your art (or writing) hand happy.

Your Website

This is a no brainer. Whichever site is hosting your comic, put your merchandise up there, too. ComicSpace and some of the other hosting services have special locations where you can post your items. You might try setting up an eBay Store (stores.ebay.com), a Yahoo Store (smallbusiness.yahoo.com), or a Google Base (www.google.com/base/). Once you've got a storefront set up at one of these sites, you can link to your items from your webcomic's location. Yahoo and eBay work easily with PayPal; Google requires a similar service called Google Payments. Once a person preorders or orders your item, you'll have a record of the purchase and can pack up and send him the item as soon as it's ready.

With a POD item or book, the POD site handles ordering and shipping for you, meaning you simply need to link to the item in question, and they take care of the rest.

It helps not to be too pushy about selling items. First and foremost, people come to your site to read your comic; they want to know about the merchandise that goes with it, but they don't want it shoved in their face. If they like you and like your webcomic, they'll buy the stuff.

Convention Sales

Conventions are important for webcomics creators. Though there are costs involved in travel, registration, lodging, and the table itself, the goal is to sell enough books and items associated with your webcomic to make back all that money and more. The other goal is to promote the hell out of your comic so you pick up devoted readers.

Note that these costs can be mitigated somewhat. Most conventions have free registration passes for professionals, so that takes care of a big chunk right there, assuming they count webcomics creators in that group.

Still other conventions, if you ask nicely or convince them (or they ask you!), will put you in as a guest, meaning that your table is taken care of and sometimes hotel and/or travel costs as well (though covering travel costs is rarer unless you're a big name). Be sure to contact the convention organizers and, in a nice way, find out how they can help cover some of your costs. You're trying to support yourself, and you definitely don't want to finish the convention in the hole.

It also helps to have at least one big convention within driving distance to save on travel and lodging costs.

Once you're signed on to a convention, it helps to promote your appearance to your fans, so that you'll have a built-in audience when you get there.

You will also want to register far enough in advance that you can order as many shirts, postcards, and books as you think you'll need. If you've already got that stuff in hand, great! You're ahead of the game.

It helps to create some professional-looking signs describing what is free and how much the stuff is that isn't free. Some creators even make a big banner that hangs behind them. It helps to look around at local copy centers and find out who can do that for you on the cheap.

Some webcomics creators make it a point to hit conventions several times a year. Moving books and merchandise at a show can often be a creator's main source of income. Plus, it's fun to get to know other creators and network with editors and publishers.

See the following sidebar for a list of conventions known to be friendly to webcomics creators.

Webcomics-Friendly Conventions

These conventions tend to have lots of webcomics creators, as the convention is friendly toward them. Look for these shows to be good opportunities to move books and merchandise. Note that if your webcomic is manga, you have about two or three times as many shows you can try. Manga/anime shows are everywhere. And some of them are friendly to non-manga as well.

Also note that these are just the big shows. Check out small to mid-size conventions in your area. They may be happy to have you.

- MegaCon. Early March. Orlando, FL. www.megaconvention.com

- Wizard World Los Angeles. Mid-March. Los Angeles, CA. www.wizardworld.com/losangeles.html

- Wizard World Philadelphia. Late May/Early June. Philadelphia, PA. www.wizardworld.com/philadelphia.html

- Museum of Comic and Cartoon Art Festival (MoCCA). Early June. New York, NY. www.moccany.org

- Wizard World Chicago. Late June. Rosemont, IL. www.wizard-world.com/chicago.html

- Comic-Con International: San Diego. Late July. San Diego, CA. www.comic-con.org

- Small Press Expo (SPX). Mid-October. Bethesda, MD. www.spxpo.com

- Alternative Press Expo (APE). Early November. San Francisco, CA. www.comic-con.org/ape/

- Wizard World Texas. Mid-November. Arlington, TX. www.wizard-world.com/texas.htm

13

The Future of Comics

Though there will always be print comics, the future of independent, creator-owned comics is on the Web. There's never been a better time to be a comic book creator than right now. Unlike the contracting indie print comics market, the already boundless opportunities for webcomics are growing every day. It's a new frontier, and though big business is starting to take notice, it's still possible for the little guy (you, in other words) to carve out your little corner of the Web and plant a webcomic there.

A Large, Untapped Audience

Many people who spend any amount of time on the Web are fans of at least one webcomic and check it regularly. Often, more people download an illegal scanned print comic book than purchase it in the store. Legions of manga fans can't wait for their favorite series to come stateside, so they translate series from Japanese to English and distribute them online—a process called *scanlation*.

In other words, the audience for webcomics is huge, increasing in age range and scope, and still largely untapped. For example, though there are many videogame webcomics out there, there aren't a whole lot of Westerns, space operas, courtroom dramas, or police procedurals. Though there's a lot of humor webcomics about tech support, there aren't a lot of webcomics about new marriages, having kids, nightclub life, or the horrors of middle school. If a skilled creator makes a webcomic about something he is passionate about, that creator could tap into a potential audience of millions.

Become Financially Self-Sufficient

At one time, there were fewer than a dozen webcomics creators supporting themselves solely from webcomics income. That number is growing daily. There are webcomics that you've probably never heard of that have managed to find their niche, grow, and support their creators. You can make it happen. In fact, the webcomics path is one of the easiest and most viable paths toward income and stability in comics. While it's true that the best of the best can get print comics work with the majors (such as Marvel and DC), it takes serious skills (which you can develop by doing webcomics, naturally), and you usually don't own your work. With webcomics, skill does count, though writing can count just as much as art. The standards are just different on the Web—creativity tends to be emphasized over pure artistic skill. Plus, creative ownership is paramount. Unless you specifically allow it, there's nobody taking a piece of the pie except you. The bottom line is that others support themselves with webcomics and so can you.

The Hardest Thing About Webcomics

The most difficult part about webcomics is not all the ancillary stuff. It's not the business end. It's not worrying about unique visitors and demographics and conventions and advertising. The hardest part about webcomics is doing it.

Get yourself in the habit, get a regular schedule, and stick to it! Start with one a week and increase in frequency if you can. The important thing is not to miss updates. Write, draw, and post your comic regularly, and you won't hamstring yourself on the way to growing an audience.

You'll also find that your writing and drawing skill increases as you go. Take a look at the early work of many popular long-running webcomics. Frankly, most of it was not very good. But they kept at it, hammering away at their craft, and got better—in some cases, quantum leaps better. And they increased their audience from a tiny close-knit group of friends into an enormous, unruly fanbase.

You can do it too. This book can help, but we can't force you to create. You have to do that on your own. You owe it to yourself to tell the kinds of stories you want to tell and fully control them in an environment where generating income is not only possible, it's being done by thousands as you're reading this.

So what are you waiting for? The future of comics is now, and it's time for you to be a part of it.

The Webcomics 2.0 Interview: The Infinite Canvas Exhibit

The Museum of Comic and Cartoon Art, also known as MoCCA, launched an art exhibit to promote webcomics at the end of 2007. By focusing purely on webcomics art, MoCCA gave webcomics even greater credibility and prominence.

This show is a symbol of webcomics' emergence. Webcomics are important, and an art exhibit devoted to them is one proof of this.

The interviewee is Jennifer Babcock, curator of the Infinite Canvas Exhibit.

WC20: How did the Infinite Canvas exhibit come about, and how did you come to be its curator?

Jennifer Babcock: I started volunteering at the Museum of Comic and Cartoon Art in February 2006 with the intention of eventually becoming one of its curators. While I was working on building the library's collection of scholarly works about comics, I asked the museum director, Matt Murray, if MoCCA had ever considered doing a webcomics exhibit. Matt, and the chief curator at the time, Bill Roundy, told me that they had, but that no one could figure out how to present a digital medium to the gallery. When I outlined some of my ideas to them, Matt and Bill decided to let me curate the exhibit. I was given the green light by the curatorial staff sometime around May.

I wanted to create an exhibit about webcomics because I feel that they contribute greatly to the comics world but are unfortunately often overlooked—especially by scholars and museums.

WC20: What are some of the goals for this exhibit? You want to show that webcomics are serious works of art?

JB: I wanted to recognize webcomics as being an integral element of the comics world and industry. Lately there have been a lot of exhibits about comics in major museums—The Hammer Museum and LA MoCCA hosted "Masters of American Comics," which later moved to the Jewish Museum in New York and the Newark Museum in New Jersey. There was also an exhibit in 2006 at NY MoMA called "Comic Abstraction," which was not particularly focused on comics, but rather how comics influence contemporary art. And by contemporary art, I'm not referring to "Pop Art" of the 1960s—I'm talking about art that is being made today.

There has been quite a buzz about comics lately, and it's been a very popular topic among scholars—Robert Storr, the dean of the art school at Yale, led a comics seminar before he left his teaching position at my art history department at NYU.

This interest is great, but I felt like webcomics were being ignored. I'm not sure if it's because people don't want to recognize their importance, or if it's because there are still a lot of people who are completely ignorant of their existence and their impact on how they've changed the way we look at comics as a whole. My former professor Robert Storr, who was also, by the way, one of the writers for the "Masters of American Comics" exhibition catalog, claimed to know nothing about them.

Anyway, I think webcomics play a huge role now and will continue to do so in the future. I wanted to show visitors why and how that is. Other than my own bias for wanting to put together this show, since I write my own webcomic, I was also thinking of the many friends I have who write webcomics for fun and the many more I know who read them. I know a lot more people who have read *Penny Arcade* or *Something Positive* than *Sandman* or *The Dark Knight Returns*—which is not to dis them, of course; they're great comics. It's just that I think webcomics are able to reach out to more people than printed comics can.

WC20: Tell me about how some of the creators involved came to be a part of the exhibit.

JB: Basically I sat down with myself, and sometimes Bill and Matt, to think of creators we wanted to be in the show—creators we thought would get our point across or were just so influential in the webcomics community that we just had to have them.

Unfortunately, some of the people we wanted to be included in the show weren't able to participate, but we did get a lot of great pieces. I'm particularly proud of our 24-foot long "infinite canvas" printout of Scott McCloud's *My Obsession with Chess.*

Basically, we wanted diverse creators whose comics could do one or more of the following: cater to a niche audience, use the infinite canvas format, create a close-knit community between different creators, or demonstrate a dialectical relationship between the creator and the audience. We also took comics that moved to print and print comics that went online.

WC20: How has the response been so far?

JB: *Wizard Magazine,* Fleen.com, and Heidi MacDonald's blog "The Beat" for *Publishers Weekly* have all given "Infinite Canvas" glowing reviews. People have really liked the way the exhibit was put together and have said that it hit on all the important spots that need to be discussed when it comes to webcomics.

This is the first paragraph of Gary Tyrell's blog, Fleen.com, after coming to the opening:

Last night, the Museum of Comics and Cartoon Art in New York City opened its latest exhibit, and for the first time webcomics made it into the world of culture and connoisseurs. I don't get to too many museum exhibition openings, but I do know one thing—when the room is packed wall-to-wall and the air conditioning is insufficient to cool the air from all the people, it's not because of the snacks or the booze. It's because people want to see the pretty stuff on the walls. By that criterion alone, the opening of "Infinite Canvas: The Art of Webcomics" would have to be judged an enormous success.

The opening was a lot more successful than I could've ever imagined it to be. Jon Rosenberg was there, and Scott McCloud was even able to drop by. It's fair to say that I was on Cloud 9 for quite some time.

In the meantime, people have been coming from all over the country to see the exhibit, which is great for MoCCA and the webcomics community.

Glossary

ACT-I-VATE Founded by Dean Haspiel and seven other cartoonists, ACT-I-VATE (act_i_vate.livejournal.com) is a mature-audiences webcomics collective on Livejournal. ACT-I-VATE is by invitation only and requires that each creator be a writer-artist. This collective is well regarded enough to have its own section in the Infinite Canvas webcomics art exhibit at the Museum of Comic and Cartoon Art.

adventure These webcomics are typified by lots of action, cliffhangers, strong characterization, and dymanic art. Super-hero webcomics would fall under the Adventure banner. Adventure is one of our chosen types of webcomics and is represented in this book by *The Drifter*.

advertising Effective use of advertising on the webcomics page can generate significant income while not distracting readers too much from the actual content. Project Wonderful (www.projectwonderful.com) is one advertising service that the webcomics community has adopted. Alternatively, the more popular webcomics are able to accept advertising directly from big-name clients. Advertising also encompasses paying for ad space on another site, which is meant to generate unique visitors and ultimately pay for itself.

archive The archives are all of your past webcomics installments, viewable in consecutive order. Some webcomics have archives that are so popular that the archive pages have their own ads with separate rates.

artist The artist is the member of the webcomics creative team responsible for drawing the project. In webcomics, the artist usually pencils and inks the project; occasionally, there's a separate penciller and inker, as in traditional print comics.

Blank Label Comics Founded in 2005, Blank Label Comics (www.blanklabelcomics.com) is an invitation-only collective originally made up of members who left the Keenspot collective. Current members include Paul Southworth (*Ugly Hill*), Paul Taylor (*Wapsi Square*), Steve Troop (*Melonpool*), David Willis (*Shortpacked!*), Greg Dean (Real Life Comics), and Howard Tayler (*Schlock Mercenary*).

blog Short for weblog, a blog is a type of website where people post about anything and everything in a sort of journal or diary format. Unlike a message board, blog communication is generally one-way, with optional comments under each post providing any return dialog. Blogs are extraordinarily popular and integrate well with webcomics for a seamless text-and-art experience.

Chemistry Set, The Launched in 2006 by Vito Delsante, a friend of the ACT-I-VATE crew, The Chemistry Set (www.chemsetcomics.com) is a writer-focused collective, and each of its webcomics has a creative team rather than a single writer-artist. Among its members are Delsante and Tom Williams (*Stuck*); Jim Dougan and various artists (*Vulture Gulch*); Chris Arrant and Dan Warner (*1 Way Ticket*); Elizabeth Genco and Adam Boorman (*Scheherazade*); Steven Goldman, Jeremy Arambulo, Dan Goldman, and Rami Efal (*Styx Taxi*); and Neil Kleid and Kevin Colden (*Todt Hill*).

Clickwheel A digital comics collective that specializes in displaying comics on cell phones and iPods, Clickwheel (www.clickwheel.net) was purchased in 2007 by Rebellion/2000AD, known for its *Judge Dredd* comics. Clickwheel is edited by Tim Demeter.

collective A collective is a term for an invitation-only webcomics site with a limited roundup of titles. The members of these collectives have different ways of recruiting or calling for submissions; check each collective's website or contact its members for more information. Some collectives are structured to generate income for their members; some collectives are done purely as a free exercise in creative expression (though these collectives have often led to print comics deals for its members).

ComicGenesis Originally known as KeenSpace, ComicGenesis (www.comicgenesis.com) is the free, all-inclusive webcomics hosting service that's a sister site to collective Keenspot. Several ComicGenesis members have graduated to Keenspot proper.

ComicPress A theme for blog software WordPress, ComicPress (www.mind-faucet.com/comicpress/) is developed and maintained by Tyler Martin, who also creates the webcomic *Wally & Osborne*. ComicPress is designed to easily integrate webcomics into a blog interface on your own website. The popular webcomic *PvP* switched to ComicPress in late 2007. To really get the most out of ComicPress, knowledge of cascading style sheets (CSS) is helpful.

ComicSpace A merging of Joey Manley's webcomics hosting service Webcomics Nation and Josh Roberts' social networking site ComicSpace, the new ComicSpace (www.comicspace.com) was relaunched in the second quarter of 2008 as an ambitious, all-in-one hosting solution for webcomics creators.

creator A creator in comics terms is the person who conceives of the idea and is usually the writer, the artist, or both. Unless the creator voluntarily gives up such rights, he has a say in anything that happens to this creation. The creator also has the right to benefit financially from it. Creator's rights were a tenuous thing for many years in the print comics world. Webcomics, which remain mostly free of corporate influence, seem to have embraced these creator's rights wholeheartedly.

DeviantArt An online art portfolio site, DeviantArt (www.deviantart.com) is a great place to go to find potential members of your webcomics creative team. It's also a good place to show off art from your webcomic and gain fans and comments.

Devil's Panties, The Not satanic porn in any way, *The Devil's Panties* (www.thedevilspanties.com) is a Keenspot comic created by Jennie Breeden. A semi-autobiographical humor strip, *The Devil's Panties* has steadily increased in popularity and has a swiftly selling print collection in stores.

DigitalWebbing A haven for independent comics creators, DigitalWebbing (www.digitalwebbing.com) is an excellent place to find collaborators for a print comic or webcomic project. Many of the people who respond to a classified ad expect money up front, and you'll get a lot of subpar responses, so it's important to hold out for the best talent.

Drifter, The Created by Steve Horton and Sam Romero, *The Drifter* is one of this book's three webcomics examples. *The Drifter* is an homage to 1970s and 1980s television detective shows, and it stars Keith Kincaid as a former New Jersey private detective who hits the road to escape a shadowy organization that wants him dead. Along with his assistant Jennifer Lancaster, Kincaid finds himself in a new location, solving a new mystery, every episode. *The Drifter*'s continuing saga can be found on www.comicspace.com.

DrunkDuck Dylan Squires founded this webcomics collective in 2002, and it was later purchased by Hollywood-focused comics company Platinum Studios. In early 2008, the interface was completely revamped. DrunkDuck (www.drunkduck.com) is best known for its active comments system and ease of use.

Dueling Analogs Created by Steve Napierski, *Dueling Analogs* (www.duelinganalogs.com) has managed to find success in a crowded field of gaming humor webcomics. Focusing exclusively on satire of games and gaming culture, *Dueling Analogs* is a favorite of many gaming news sites and has been featured in print in *Hardcore Gamer Magazine*.

Edge the Devilhunter Created by Sam Romero, *Edge the Devilhunter* is the second of three webcomics examples in this book. *Edge the Devilhunter* is hard-edged manga and stars the title character as a morally ambiguous assassin. *Edge the Devilhunter* has been remastered for the short story at the center of this book, and the complete archives can be found at www.graphicsmash.com/comics/edgethedevilhunter.php.

FTP FTP stands for File Transfer Protocol, and it's a way to transfer large files from one place to another. In webcomics terms, FTP is most often used to deliver webcomics to the hosting service or collective. One good, easy-to-use FTP program is CoreFTP at www.coreftp.com.

Girl Genius A "gaslamp" fantasy comic that began life in print before becoming much more successful as a webcomic, *Girl Genius* (www.girlgeniusonline.com) is created by longtime comics veterans Phil and Kaja Foglio.

hosting service A webcomics hosting service is a website where anyone can sign up and post webcomics. An invitation or application is not required. Similar to MySpace and YouTube in that it is a completely creative, do-it-yourself enterprise, which is what the Web 2.0 concept is all about. The most ambitious of all hosting services is ComicSpace (www.comicspace.com), but it is far from the only choice.

humor A majority of popular webcomics are humor based. Humor webcomics find specific things to be funny about and attract an audience of fans who share the comics among themselves. The humor in webcomics can be far too edgy and adult for newspaper comics; however, many humor webcomics have made their way into print comics or print book collections and have found much success that way.

infinite canvas Coined by Scott McCloud in his book *Reinventing Comics*, infinite canvas is the concept that webcomics need not follow a traditional print model, but can use the entire landscape of a webpage for ultimate creativity. Those webcomics that choose to utilize infinite canvas can go in any direction on the page and have any size panels. Infinite canvas webcomics can run into problems when adapted for print, but the point of this concept is to use the Web to its utmost; translations into other media are a secondary concern.

installment An installment is a single webcomic page, panel, or sequence that's posted as one entity on a specific update day. If your webcomic updates three times a week, that's three installments.

intellectual property A legal term for your webcomics creation. The webcomics industry, in general, is set up such that each creator retains control of his intellectual property, and thus everyone has the chance to benefit, rather than a select few.

Keenspot One of the first webcomics collectives, Keenspot (www.keenspot.com) was founded in March 2000 by Chris Crosby, Darren Bleuel, and others and has hosted some of the most popular webcomics. Many of those webcomics have eventually gone independent or joined other collectives, while others have chosen to remain with the Keenspot fold. Among the most popular current Keenspot webcomics are *The Devil's Panties*, by Jennie Breeden, *Sore Thumbs*, by Crosby and Owen Gieni, and *Clan of the Cats*, by Jamie Robertson.

Livejournal Livejournal (www.livejournal.com) is one of the most popular blogging sites on the Internet. Its sense of community is strong enough that it has spawned several webcomics collectives that use Livejournal as a base of operations. Perhaps the most well-known of these is ACT-I-VATE.

manga   Literally, Japanese for comics, manga is simultaneously a style, a medium, and a genre. Many webcomics are drawn in a manga style. One reason for this is because anime, Japanese for animation, dominates television, and manga dominates the graphic novel section of bookstores. Manga is also one of three types of webcomics chosen for this book and is represented by *Edge the Devilhunter*.

merchandise   Ultimately, a webcomics creator can make more from merchandise than the webcomic itself. This is not selling out, as the webcomics creator retains control of his creation. Rather, it's using the intellectual property in an effective way and giving fans a tangible object to remind them of your webcomic. Merchandise can take the form of T-shirts and other apparel, book collections, posters and prints, and more.

Modern Tales   Modern Tales, founded by Joey Manley, is an umbrella of webcomics collectives (Modern Tales, Girlamatic, Serializer, and Graphic Smash) that originally attempted the subscription model before going free. It's unclear as of press time how the Modern Tales family will integrate into the new ComicSpace hosting service, but it seems that being invited to a Modern Tales site will still be beneficial.

Megatokyo   Created by Fred Gallagher and Rodney Caston and currently produced by Gallagher solo, *Megatokyo* (www.megatokyo.com) is a manga-style webcomic originally done as a humor strip before morphing into a relationship drama. *Megatokyo* remains one of the most popular webcomics in existence and currently has multiple reprint volumes available from DC Comics' CMX manga imprint. According to icv2.com, *Megatokyo* is the most popular OEL (original English language) manga.

MySpace   In a close race with Facebook as the most popular social networking site, MySpace (www.myspace.com) is a great place to go to promote a webcomic. A well-designed and non-garish MySpace page can be a good way to spread the word about news, post blogs (though the blog interface isn't the greatest), and post extras. MySpace's new comics page, MySpace Comics, shows that the site is serious about the subject.

non sequitur   Latin for "it doesn't follow," non sequitur or off-the-wall is a type of webcomic where unpredictability and chaos reign. Anything can happen at any time, and often a non sequitur webcomic will go for weirdness rather than the joke but make people laugh nonetheless.

pageviews One way of measuring a webcomic's popularity, this number tracks how many times the pages on your webcomics site are viewed. A more accurate measurement, though, is unique visitors.

panel Bounded by a square, circle, or other shape, a webcomics panel is a single storytelling instance. Webcomics can have as few as one panel and theoretically an infinite number of panels. In a practical sense, webcomics usually contain three to seven panels per installment.

Panel and Pixel A website created by Rantz Hoseley to give the community of Warren Ellis' defunct *The Engine* a home, Panel and Pixel (www.panelandpixel.com) is one of the few places where comics creators interact with each other and with fans in a civil and professional manner. Some of the brightest stars in print comics and webcomics post frequently here, and real names are required. There's a section where only published creators can post and a few others that only creators can even see, but even those still breaking in will find a lot of useful information here.

PencilJack An artist-focused website with active forums, PencilJack (www.penciljack.com) is a good place to find paying work and to find good artists. Most of the artists here, as on similar site DigitalWebbing, expect to be paid up front, so keep that in mind.

Penny and Aggie Created by T Campbell and Gisele Lagace, *Penny and Aggie* (www.pennyandaggie.com) is a relationship drama that appeared on the Keenspot collective before striking out on its own. Recently, *Penny and Aggie* collections were made available on the Wowio e-book download service, to much success.

Penny Arcade If you ask a random passerby what he thinks of when he thinks of webcomics, odds are he'll say *Penny Arcade* (www.penny-arcade.com). The popularity of this videogame humor strip, created by Jerry Holkins and Mike Krahulik, is into the stratosphere. *Penny Arcade* now employs a business manager, Robert Khoo, and a small staff and is responsible for the Child's Play children's hospital charity and the Penny Arcade Expo, a gaming culture convention. *Penny Arcade* has also spawned its own videogame and collectible trading-card game and a best-selling series of books from Dark Horse Comics. *Penny Arcade* isn't just a webcomic—it's an empire.

press release A press release is a letter written in a specific format for a news organization, which either posts the press release verbatim or adapts it into a news story. Press releases are key for getting out important news relating to your webcomic. Many of the most popular comics news sites will run a press release, provided it's presented to them in a professional manner.

Project Wonderful Created by Ryan North of Dinosaur Comics fame, Project Wonderful (www.projectwonderful.com) is an innovative advertising auction website that's been embraced by the webcomics community. By combining the bidding features of a site like eBay with tools for buying and selling ad space, creators can both purchase ad space on popular sites and sell ad space on their own sites, increasing their traffic and income in the process.

promotion Promotion is the effort you take to get the word out about your webcomic. Promotion should be done through correct channels, as unwanted promotion can be labeled spam and get you bad publicity. Some good avenues of promotion are press releases, signature files, appropriate places in message boards, and through purchasing ad space on another site.

PvP Created by Scott Kurtz, *PvP* (www.pvponline.com), which stands for Player vs. Player, is an extraordinarily popular pop-culture humor strip. Originally focusing on gaming humor, *PvP* has expanded into more general comedy in recent years. *PvP* has spawned a comic book and trade paperback series from Image Comics and a Web animated series, produced by Ferret Entertainment. This animated series is also available on the Xbox Live service.

Questionable Content One of the Web's most interesting webcomics examples in the slice-of-life genre, *Questionable Content* (www.questionablecontent.net), created by Jeph Jacques, combines elements of independent rock music humor with relationship drama. Mixed in to this is humor and drama about many other subjects. *Questionable Content* has a huge, devoted audience and is one of the few popular webcomics that has stayed independent (i.e., not affiliated with any collective or service) since its inception.

revenue-generating object As defined in this book, a revenue-generating object is something related to but apart from the webcomic itself that generates income and helps you continue to create. Merchandise is an example of a revenue-generating object.

RSS RSS stands for Really Simple Syndication. It's an Internet invention that allows someone using an RSS reader to collect news and headlines from many websites into one place. RSS is important for webcomics because it allows people to be reminded when a webcomic (and the corresponding blog post) has updated. Most Web browsers have an RSS reader built in.

script Comics writers write in a specific script format tailored for an artist. This script format closely resembles but is not identical to scripts written for television and movies. Comics scripts contain panel-by-panel descriptions of the events in an installment and also include the dialogue, captions, and sound effects that the letterer will later provide.

self-publishing As defined in this book, self-publishing refers to avoiding webcomics collectives and hosting services and publishing on your own website. This requires knowing a bit about Web design and the use of MySQL and PHP. Designing your own website is significantly less difficult today than yesterday; although self-publishing is not trivial, it's not extraordinarily difficult, either.

Shortpacked! Created by David Willis as a continuation of his Walkyverse stories, started by *Roomies* and *It's Walky!* and continuing in parallel with *Joyce* and *Walky*, *Shortpacked!* (www.shortpacked.com) is a humor strip about the offbeat employees at a toy store. *Shortpacked!* is part of the Blank Label Comics collective and is perhaps the most popular webcomic there.

slice of life A slice-of-life webcomic is one that's primarily concerned with everyday life and avoids fantastical elements as much as possible. These webcomics are a dramatic interpretation of everyday life. Slice-of-life webcomics have characters that grow and develop over months and years, and readers can become quite emotionally invested in them.

strip A less precise way to say *installment*, a strip is a single webcomic. Installment is more correct because only a segment of webcomics are drawn in a horizontal, or strip format. This terminology is carried over from newspapers, where nearly all comics are strips.

subscription model The subscription model was one attempt at pay for webcomics creators, whereby users would pay a monthly fee and gain access to high-quality webcomics. The reason the subscription model failed for webcomics is the same reason it failed for most websites in general: People are used to getting their Web content free, and thus alternative means of creator payment must be devised. The few webcomics collectives that have tried the subscription model (such as Modern Tales) eventually abandoned that model for an advertiser-supported free model, which fits better in today's Web 2.0 era.

unique visitors When tracking statistics on your webcomics site, the number of unique visitors is one of the most important elements to follow. This measurement tracks a specific person on a specific computer and counts that person only once. Therefore, unique visitors measures how many different actual people, not clicks or hits, visit your site in the given time interval. Rising unique visitors is a good sign that your webcomic is becoming more popular.

Versus Verses, The Created and written by T Campbell and drawn by Sam Romero, *The Versus Verses* is the third webcomics example in this book and is an example of the humor genre. A satire of popular culture, *The Versus Verses* is a mashup of two pop-culture characters that happen to rhyme with each other. As the characters come into conflict, they rhyme with each other. *The Versus Verses* debuts in the pages of this book and continues at ComicSpace.com.

Web, the Short for the World Wide Web, the Web is the graphical component of the Internet, expressed in HTML and other languages. The Web is the vehicle by which webcomics are delivered to readers.

Web 2.0 A nickname for the trend of user-creativity among websites, Web 2.0 refers to sites such as YouTube and MySpace that allow users themselves to contribute to, shape, and control the content. Webcomics predated Web 2.0, but they fit naturally within the concept. Webcomics are a true do-it-yourself creative enterprise. The title of this book is a portmanteau, or mashup, of Web 2.0 and webcomics.

Webcomic Comics that are published on the Web are webcomics. Webcomics need not be exclusive to or originate on the Web; in fact, many print comics have found new life as reprints and original series on the Web. Conversely, many webcomics have found new venues in bookstores and comic shops as reprint collections.

Wowio Wowio (www.wowio.com) is a free e-book download site with a massive library of comics. Though many of these comics are digital reprints of print comics, several are collected editions of webcomics. Downloads are free, and creators get paid due to sponsorship deals with Verizon and CareerBuilder.

writer The writer is the member of the webcomics creative team who writes the project. Often, but not always, the writer comes up with the initial concept for the webcomic. Webcomics writers usually write in comic script format because it is a standard method that helps the artist visualize what he is about to draw.

writer-artist Many webcomics are created by a single person who writes and draws the entire thing. This is beneficial because one person gets to keep all the money and has an easier time making a living. Also, a single person's creative vision can be said to be purer than a team's.

Index

A

Abram, Pete, 6
action, rising, 107
ACT-I-VATE, 161
ads. *See also* promotion
  formatting, 171–173
  Google AdWords, 180–182
  Project Wonderful, 170–179
Adsense, Google, 181, 184–185
ad space, buying, 170–181
adventure webcomics, 2
  Drifter, The, 20–34
  overview of, 19–20
advertising, 184. *See also*
  promotion
AdWords, Google, 180–182
Alvin and the Chipmunks, 15
Amazon.com, BookSurge, 189
American Splendor, 47
Another Fine Myth, 132
AOL, 13
Apple products, 200
approaches to writing, 104
Archaia Studios, 10
archives, downloadable, 142
arcs, story, 105
Arrant, Chris, 150–153

art, 113–114. *See also* drawing
  borders, 133
  character profiles, 135
  colors, 123–126
  drafts, 118–120
  extras, 134
  finishing, 123
  full bleed, 133–134
  iced ink, 121
  lettering, 126–132
  panel borders, 118
  saving, 133
  scanning, 121–122
  scripts, studying, 117–118
  thumbnails, 117
Asprin, Robert, 132
audience for webcomics, 209
autobiography, humor webcomics,
  9–12

B

Babcock, Jennifer, 211–214
balloons. *See* text
banners, 170. *See also* ads
Berlin, 151
bids, placing, 173–175
black areas, applying, 121

Blambot fonts, 128
Blank Label Comics, 6, 9, 13, 148
bleed, 133
Bleuel, Darren, 146
blogs as promotional tools, 160–161
books, 189–193. *See also* publishing
    promotional tours, 169
BookSurge, 189
borders
    art, 133
    panels, 118
Brady, Matt, 164
Brawl, 152
Breeden, Jennie, 9–12
Brunetto, Kurt, 188
brushes, 122
Buck Godot, 132

C

Calvin & Hobbes, 15
campaigns, 175–176
Campbell, T., 50–51, 61
captions, 96, 126–132
careers, 60
Cartoon Network, 52
cascading style sheets. *See* CSS
Caston, Rodney, 36, 53
CBR/CBZ format, 199
CDisplay, 199
Chabon, Michael, 47
characters
    bibles, writing, 94–95
    character driven storytelling, 104
    Drifter, The, 20–34
    Edge the Devilhunter, 37–45
    manga, 36
    profiles, 135

Chemistry Set, The, 150–153
Civilization IV: Beyond the Sword, 5
ClickWheel, 193, 199, 200–202
close on, 96
CMYK (cyan, magenta, yellow, black), 123–126
Cody, Jasmine, 40
collaboration, 117
collectives, 146–153
    ACT-I-VATE, 149
    Blank Label Comics, 148
    Chemistry Set, The, 150–153
    Dayfree Press, 177
    Halfpixel, 148
    Keenspot, 146
    Modern Tales, 149
coloring art, 123–126
combining webcomic types, 53
Comflix, 146
Comic Abstraction, 212
Comic Book Resources, 164
ComicGenesis, 144
comic news and commentary sites, 164
ComicPress, 155
Comic Sans fonts, 128
Comics Bulletin, 164
comic scripts, writing, 96–103
ComicSpace, 143
    promotion on, 160
comic strips, 1
ComixTalk, 167
comments as promotional tools, 162
communication, 59
consignment, 168
Contino, Jennifer, 164

conventions
  list of, 208
  sales, 207–208
  signings, 168–169
Cook, Nikki, 151
Cool Cat Studio, 50
CoreFTP, 140
cost
  of book and convention signings,
    170
  low-cost promotion, 168–181
  no-cost promotion, 158–167
  of print runs, 192
courtroom dramas, 209
creative teams, 55, 57
  sole creators, 55–56
  talent, finding, 58–60
credibility, 211
Crosby, Chris, 146–148
CSS (cascading style sheets), 155
customizing hosting services, 142
cut to, 96
cyan, magenta, yellow, black. *See*
  CMYK

D

Damn Good Comics, 167
Dark Horse Comics, 4, 52, 192
Dark Knight Returns, The, 212
Dayfree Press, 177
DC Comics, 203
Dean, Greg, 9, 148
Delsante, Vito, 150–153
Demeter, Tim, 200–202
denouement, 107
descriptions, characters, 94–95
development. *See* creative teams

Devil's Panties, The, 9–12
dialogue, 128. *See also* lettering
DigitalWebing, 158
Dinosaur Comics, 52, 166, 177
Disquietville, 204
Doberman, The, 153
documents, PDF (Portable
  Document Format), 193–199
downloadables, 193–205
  archives, 142
drafts, art, 118–120
dragging and dropping files, FTP,
  140–141
drawing
  improving, 114
  skills, 210–214
  webcomics, 114–117
Drifter, The, 20–34, 61
  scripts, writing, 96–103
Drilon, Andrew, 152
DriveThruComics, 193, 194–196
DrunkDuck, 144–145, 184
Dueling Analogs, 4, 5–6

E

Edge (a.k.a. "Jack"), 37–39. *See also*
  manga
Edge the Devilhunter, 37–45, 62
  evolution of, 135–137
electronic lettering, 126–132
Ellerton, Sarah, 111–111
e-mail, 59
  press releases, 163
establishing shot, 96
examples of webcomics, 62–91
extras,art, 134

F

faces, 116
Fans, 51
farms, servers, 154
FCHS, 153
Fiffe, Michael, 149
files. *See also* art
    FTP, 140–141
    importing, 121
File Transfer Protocol. *See* FTP
financial self-sufficiency, achieving, 210
finishing art, 123
finite book pages, 134
Firaxis Games, 5
flashbacks, 109
Flash Gordon, 19
Fleen, 166, 213
Foglio, Kaja, 131
Foglio, Phil, 131
fonts, 126–128. *See also* lettering
formatting
    ads, 171–173
    art, 134
    CBR/CBZ format, 199
    half-page formats, 203
    PDF, 193–199
forums, promotion, 158
Foundation, 8
Foxymoron, 204
frames, 96
Friends, 47
FTP (File Transfer Protocol), 140–141
Fugitive, The, 20
full bleed art, 133–134
future of webcomics, 209–214

G

gag-a-day webcomics, 105
Gallagher, Fred, 36, 53
Gigcast: The Webcomics Podcast, 164
Girl Genius, 131
Girls with Slingshots, 10
Gloom, The, 153
G-Man, 27–34, 95. *See also* adventure webcomics
GoComics, 203–205
GoDaddy, 154
Goldman, Steven, 150–153
Google
    AdSense, 180, 184–185
    AdWords, 180–182
Graphic Smash, 149
Grey's Anatomy, 47
Grounded Angel, 162
Gurewitch, Nicholas, 52

H

half-page formats, 203
Halfpixel collective, 148
Hammer Museum, 212
hard coding, 155
Harry Potter, 15
Haspiel, Dean, 149
Hernanadez, Gilbert, 151
Herobear, 10
Holkins, Jerry, 4, 57
Hornby, Nick, 47
Horton, Steve, 61, 159, 164

hosting services, 142–145
  ComicGenesis, 144
  ComicSpace, 143
  CoreFTP, 140
  DrunkDuck, 144–145
  LiveJournal, 145
  self-publishing, selecting for, 154
Howard, Robert, 164
humor webcomics, 2
  autobiography, 9–12
  overview of, 3
  pop culture, 12–15
  science fiction, 6–9
  Versus Verses, The, 15–18
  video games, 4–6
  writing, 94

I

iced ink, 121
Immortal, 152
importing files, 121
Incredible Hulk, The, 20
Indiana Daily Student, 13
infinite canvas, 134
Infinite Canvas Exhibit, 211–214
ink, 115
  iced, 121
instant messaging, 59
Internet, 1
interviews, 167
  writing, 111–111
Inverloch, 111–111
investments in merchandise, 187
iPhone, 200
iPod, 200
It's Walky!, 13

J

Jacques, Jeph, 48–49
Japan, 205. *See also* manga
Joyce & Walky, 13
Judge Dredd, 199, 201

K

Kare-Kare Komiks, 152
Keenspot, 6, 13, 144
Kelly, Walt, 128
keywords, Google Adwords, 181
Khoo, Robert, 57
Kincaid, Pete, 21–24, 95. *See also* adventure webcomics
Kings Feature Syndicate, 50
Kingsley, Jason, 200
Koelbl, Matt, 164
Krahulik, Mike, 4, 57
Kurtz, Scott, 4, 148

L

Lagace, Gisele, 50–51
Lancaster, Jennifer, 25–27, 95. *See also* adventure webcomics
lettering, 126–132
LiveJournal, 145, 160–161
logos, 96
Lord of the Rings, 105
low-cost promotion, 168–181
Lowe, Johnny, 126–132
Lulu, 189

M

MacDonald, Heidi, 213
MacGyver, 20
MacPherson, Dwight, 150–153
Magnum P.I., 20
manga, 2
   characters, 36
   Edge the Devilhunter, 37–45
   OEL (original English language),
      46
   overview of, 35–36
   reading, 205
Manley, Joey, 143
Martin, Tyler, 155
Maus, 47
McCloud, Scott, 213, 214
McDuffie, Dwayne, 57
McNeil, Brian, 8
mechanical pencils, 120. *See also*
   drawing
Megatokyo, 36, 53, 192
Melonpool, 6, 148
merchandise, 186–189
Miller, Steve, 197–199
mobile devices, webcomics for,
   199–205
MoCCA (Museum of Comic and
   Cartoon Art), 211–214
Modern Tales, 149
money, making. *See* revenue
multiple uploads, 142
Museum of Comic and Cartoon
   Art. *See* MoCCA
My Obsession with Chess, 213
MySpace, promotion on, 158–159
Myth Adventures, 132

N

Napierski, Steve, 4, 5–6
navigating FTP programs, 140–141
News Wire, 164
no-cost promotion, 158–167
non-sequitur webcomics, 52
Norm, The, 203
North, Ryan, 52, 177–179

O

OEL (original English language),
   46
off the wall webcomics, 52
OhNoRobot, 177
original English language. *See also*
   OEL
Outer Circle, The, 6

P

pages, finite book, 134
Palomar, 151
Panel and Pixel, 158
panels, 96
   borders, 118
Panorama, 152
PayPal, 196. *See also* revenue
PDF (Portable Document Format),
   193–199
pencil drawings, 118–120
Penny and Aggie, 47, 50–51, 198
Penny Arcade, 4, 5, 192, 212
Phoenix Requiem, The, 111–111
Platinum Comics, 144
plots, 108. *See also* writing

Pogo, 128

point of view, 96

police procedurals, 209

pop culture, humor webcomics, 12–15

Popio, Nick, 190–191

Portable Document Format. *See* PDF

Powell, Nate, 151

power of the press, 163–167

presale merchandise, 186

press, power of the, 163–167

press releases, 163–166

Princess Tail (a.k.a. Jasmine Cody), 40

print on demand
  books, 189–192
  merchandise, 186

print runs, cost of, 192

profiles, characters, 135

Project Wonderful, 170–179, 185

promotion, 157
  ad space, buying, 170–181
  book tours, 169
  low-cost, 168–181
  no-cost, 158–167
  power of the press, 163–167
  Project Wonderful, 170–179

protocols, FTP (File Transfer Protocol), 140–141

publishers, signing with, 192

Publisher's Weekly, 213

publishing, 139
  collectives, 146–153
  FTP (File Transfer Protocol), 140–141
  hosting services, 142–145
  self-publishing, 154–155
  webcomics. *See* publishing

PvP, 4, 203

Q

Questionable Content, 47, 48–49

R

Ramsoomair, Scott, 4

Real Life Comics, 9, 148

Really Simple Syndication. *See* RSS

Rebellion, 200

red, green, blue. *See* RGB

references, 96

retailers, store signings, 168–169

revenue
  books, 189–193
  downloadables, 193–205
  financial self-sufficiency, achieving, 210
  merchandise, 186–189
  revenue-generating locations, 206–208
  revenue-generating objects, 184–205
  sharing, 142

reviews, 166–167

RGB (red, green, blue), 123–126

rising action, 107
Roberts, Josh, 143
Rockford Files, The, 20
Romero, Sam, 22, 26, 61
    webcomics, drawing, 114–117
Roomies!, 13
Rosenberg, Jon, 214
RSS (Really Simple Syndication), 142
Runaways, 10

S

Sandman, 212
satire, 15–18. *See also* humor webcomics
saving art, 133
scanlation, 209
scanning art, 121–122
Schlock Mercenary, 6, 7–9, 148
science fiction, humor webcomics, 6–9
scripts
    art, studying to determine, 117–118
    writing, 96–103, 116
self-publishing, 154–155
Serializer, 149
server farms, 154
services
    hosting, 142–145
SFX (sound effects), 96
sharing revenue, 142
Shortpacked!, 12–15, 53, 148
signings, 168–169
Simon, Kris, 151
Simons, Will, 200
Simpsons, The, 5

Sipe, Harold, 203–205
skills, drawing and writing, 210–214
slice of life webcomics, 47–51
Sluggy Freelance, 6
Smashout Comics, 159
Sokoliwski, Ian, 123–126
sole creators, 55–56
Something Positive, 212
sound effects (SFX), 96, 126–132
Space Ghost Coast to Coast, 52
space operas, 209
speech balloons, 126–132
Spenser: For Hire, 20
Spirit, The, 19
Spurgeon, Tom, 164
Squires, Dylan, 144
Star Trek, 6
Star Wars, 6
statistics, 177–179
Steve Canyon, 19
store signings, 168–169
Storr, Robert, 212
story arc, 105
story driven writing, 104
Straub, Kristofer, 6
structure, writing, 104–108
    approaches to, 104
    flashbacks, 109
    rising action, 107
    story arc, 105
    subplots, 108
    three act structure, 106–107
Styx Taxi, 153
subplots, 108
Surreal Adventures of Edgar Allan Poo, The, 150–153, 192

T

talent, finding, 58–60
Tangents, 167
Taylor, Howard, 6, 7–9, 148
Taylor, Paul, 148
teams. *See* creative teams
Terry and the Pirates, 19
text, 126–132
    PDF (Portable Document Format), 193–199
three act structure, 106–107
thumbnails, 117
Tiny Giants, 151
TokyoPop, 204
tools, 115
    brushes, 122
    panel creation, 118
Too Much Coffee Man, 203
tours, book, 169
transitions, writing, 110
Troop, Steve, 6
T-shirts, 187–188
types of webcomics, 2, 47–53
Tyrell, Gary, 164, 166, 213

U

Ugly Hill, 148
Universal Press Syndicate, 203
uploads, multiple, 142

V

Valentino, Jim, 151
V-CASR network, 146
Versus Verses, The, 15–18, 61
VG Cats, 4
video games, humor webcomics, 4–6

W

Wapsi Square, 10, 148
Warner Bros. Studio Store, 13
1 Way Ticket, 152
Web 2.0, 1
webcomics
    drawing, 114–117
    examples, 62–91
    future of, 209–214
    for mobile devices, 199–205
    transitions, 110
    types of, 2, 47–53
web hosts, selecting, 154
websites, 206
    talent, finding, 60
Welcome Back Kotter, 15
westerns, 209
Wieck, Steve, 194–196
Wikipedia, 8
Willis, David, 12–15, 53, 148
Wings of Juano Diaz, The, 151
Wizard Magazine, 213

Wolfit, Sire Donald, 94

Wowio, 193, 197–199

writing, 93

    character bibles, 94–95

    comic scripts, 96–103

    humor webcomics, 94

    interviews, 111–111

    lettering, 126–132

    skills, 210–214

    structure, 104–108

        approaches to, 104

        flashbacks, 109

        rising action, 107

        story arc, 105

        subplots, 108

        three act structure, 106–107

    transitions, 110

www.deviantar.com, 60

www.digitalwebbing.com, 60

www.panelandpixel.com, 60

www.penciljack.com, 60

X

Xerexes, Xaviar, 164

xkcd, 12

Z

Zelda the Goth (a.k.a. Zelda Ricci), 41–45. *See also* **manga**

Zuda Comics, 203